ART AND FIESTA
IN MEXICO CITY

---

*An insider's guide to the best places
to eat, drink and explore*

CRISTINA ALONSO

Hardie Grant

TRAVEL

ART AND FIESTA IN MEXICO CITY

*An insider's guide to the best places
to eat, drink and explore*

CRISTINA ALONSO

CONTENTS

WELCOME TO MEXICO CITY

Hola!

When I was little, I never gave much thought to the fact that I was growing up in Mexico City. I remember knowing that my city was huge, sure. And field trips in school meant that we'd go to places like Museo Nacional de Antropología to check out an immense amount of pre-Hispanic treasures. But I guess that, like most kids, I just took it for granted. It wasn't until I was a little older, and I was lucky enough to travel with my family, that I was able to see other amazing places – Rome! Amsterdam! – and realise, wow, my city's pretty fantastic, too.

Now, I don't believe in fate, but I do think that things have worked out pretty well since then, both for me and for the city. For one, Mexico City has undergone a fascinating transformation. While it has always been buzzing with culture – it was founded by the Aztecs in 1325 AD, so it's never lacked for history – the past few years have brought a new wave of creativity on all fronts. Young designers, artists, chefs, bartenders ... it seems like there's inspiration in every corner of this city. And I, on the other hand, was lucky enough to turn my passion for travelling into a full-time job as a travel writer and editor. So whether you're here to eat fantastic food, to get lost in a colourful market, or to delve into our cultural landscape – or hopefully, all of the above – you'll find plenty of spots to explore in the city's many interesting neighbourhoods.

I hope you enjoy every minute of your trip as much as I enjoyed working on this book. It's my privilege to guide you along your trip to this incredible, diverse – if sometimes chaotic – city.

Cristina

ABOUT
MEXICO CITY

The history of Mexico City goes back centuries and centuries: the first evidence of human population in the region can be traced back to somewhere around the year 9000 BC; then the Aztecs came and founded the great city of Tenochtitlan in 1325; and Mexico City, as capital of the New Spain, was founded in 1521 AD.

During colonial times, the city was mostly concentrated around Centro Histórico but it continued to expand over the following decades. Today, it has around nine million inhabitants, but, if we consider the whole Valley of Mexico Metropolitan Area (which also includes certain parts of the state of Mexico), it adds up to a whopping 22 million people.

A notable time in the city's history was Porfirio Diaz's presidency (1877–80 and 1884–1911), during which he commissioned several of the most iconic constructions, such as Palacio de Bellas Artes and the Angel of Independence.

These different time periods make the city a multi-layered metropolis, whose very streets and works of architecture have witnessed not only a long, complex past, but also an exciting present. This also means that there are enough cultural attractions and historic sites to satisfy even the most demanding and curious travellers.

A fertile ground for artists, Mexico City provides endless inspiration. You'll be witness to this buzz of creativity beyond the city's museums and galleries, as you explore traditional markets and boutiques by cutting-edge designers. The city's wide and eclectic culinary scene allows you to try traditional Mexican dishes, high-brow tasting menus and delicious street snacks, all in one day.

And before we dive in, let's go back to a certain detail: yes, the city has expanded significantly and it has hundreds of neighbourhoods. However, most of the highlights are concentrated in certain areas, and we've grouped the attractions by neighbourhood to make your trip as easy and stress-free as possible. So, welcome, and now go out and explore!

About

MEXICO CITY

Key

1. Museo Soumaya
2. Museo Jumex
3. Museo Nacional de Antropología
4. Chapultepec Castle
5. Museo de Arte Moderno
6. Museo del Objeto del Objeto (MODO)
7. Monumento a la Revolución (MRM)
8. Palacio de Bellas Artes
9. Museo Nacional de Arte (MUNAL)
10. Plaza de la Constitución (Zócalo) & Catedral Metropolitana
11. Museo del Templo Mayor
12. Museo Frida Kahlo

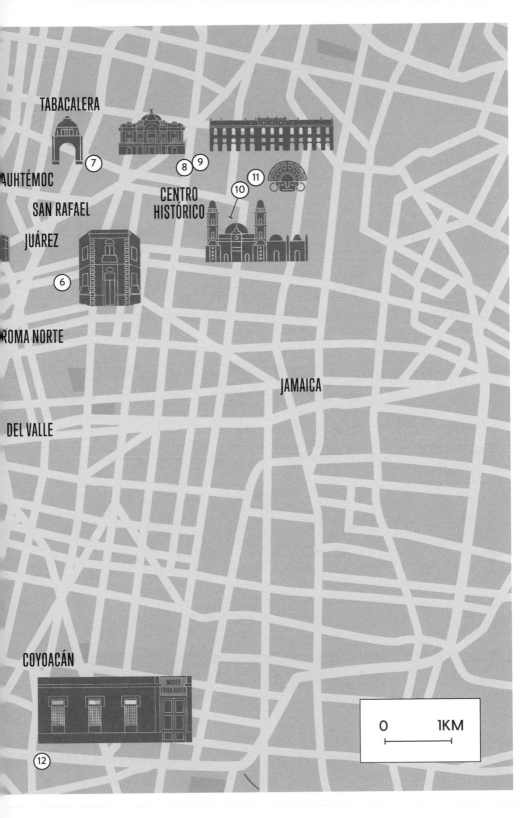

TABACALERA

CUAUHTÉMOC

SAN RAFAEL

JUÁREZ

CENTRO
HISTÓRICO

ROMA NORTE

JAMAICA

DEL VALLE

COYOACÁN

MUSEO
FRIDA KAHLO

⑥ ⑦ ⑧ ⑨ ⑩ ⑪ ⑫

0   1KM

NEIGHBOURHOOD INDEX

NEIGHBOURHOOD INDEX

Neighbourhood Index

NOTABLE
NEIGHBOURHOODS

Don't let the city's size intimidate you. The sprawling capital of Mexico is divided into 16 alcaldías, or mayoralties, which, in turn, are divided into hundreds of neighbourhoods. While it's impossible to include all of them here, this is a brief guide to the ones that feature attractions included in this book. We have ordered all venues in every chapter by these neighbourhoods, too, making it easy for you to travel around the city.

ROMA NORTE

Built in the early 20th century as a residential area, this neighbourhood still has many of the gorgeous mansions from those days. Over the past couple of decades, it has become a hotspot for culture and creativity, and its high concentration of restaurants – including neighbourhood pioneer Contramar (see p.55), beloved for its seafood, and newcomers like the breezy Meroma (see p.61) – bars, stores, boutique hotels, and art galleries – don't miss OMR (see p.161), set in a cool Brutalist building – makes it a favourite among locals and visitors alike. You'll notice that many of these businesses are actually set inside repurposed townhouses, giving them a touch of retro elegance.

CENTRO HISTÓRICO

The city's oldest neighbourhood, a UNESCO World Heritage Site, holds a history lesson in every corner. There are pre-Hispanic, Spanish colonial and modern buildings; hotels, department stores, bars and restaurants, and a great number of museums and cultural sites to admire. The area's centerpiece is Zócalo (see p.143), the city's main square, around which you'll find other attractions, like Catedral Metropolitana and Museo del Templo Mayor (see p.135), the main temple of the Mexicas in the city. This neighbourhood is also one of the busiest parts of town, always filled with visitors and locals going about their day.

NOTABLE NEIGHBOURHOODS

JUÁREZ

One of the most rapidly changing neighbourhoods in the city, Juárez begins at the border of Centro Histórico and reaches Bosque de Chapultepec park at the other end. Its origins go back to the early 20th century, which is why it has plenty of beautiful mansions. The section called Zona Rosa offers plenty of LGBTIQ+ friendly bars and clubs, and you'll also notice lots of tall office buildings, especially lined along Paseo de la Reforma. Walk along the smaller streets to find some of the newer, most interesting spots in the area, like the cosy Café Nin (see p.81) and menswear store Casa Caballería (see p.197), on Havre, or the casual Cicatriz cafe (see p.76), on Dinamarca.

CONDESA

The tree-lined streets of this neighbourhood – built on what used to be a horse racing track, el Hipódromo de la Condesa Miravalle – make it a favourite among artsy types and young families. Stroll through its lovely parks, Parque México and Parque España, and let the afternoon pass you by in hangouts like Tomás (see p.47), heaven for tea lovers, or the intimate Baltra (see p.123), where you'll find a solid menu of sophisticated cocktails. Check out its Art Deco buildings, a testimony to its heyday during the '20s and '30s.

POLANCO

Neighbouring Bosque de Chapultepec park, this is one of the loveliest areas in the city. Parts of it are purely residential, while others, like Parque Lincoln and its surrounding streets, are filled with stores, coffee shops and other businesses. Two of the city's top fine-dining destinations are in this neighbourhood: Pujol (see p.93) and Quintonil (see p.91). Along Presidente Masaryk, you will find luxury brands, as well as interesting shops like the concept store Ikal (see p.202). Many luxury hotels are also located here.

BOSQUE DE CHAPULTEPEC

We like to say that this massive park is 'the city's lungs'. Chapultepec covers 678 hectares (1675 acres) and is divided into three sections. Here, you'll find lakes, a zoo and some of the country's major museums, like Museo Nacional de Antropología (see p.147) and Museo Tamayo (see p.173). It's also an excellent option for a workout. To run or jog in its track, called El Sope, enter through Avenida de los Compositores in Section II of the park.

NOTABLE NEIGHBOURHOODS

CUAUHTÉMOC

This large neighbourhood sits across from Juárez, right on the other side of Reforma. It's also home to skyscrapers, luxury hotels and early 20th-century mansions, as well as a new wave of dining and nightlife options, including the sleek Tokyo Music Bar (see p.127) and the fun, cantina-style Salón Ríos (see p.94).

COYOACÁN

The entire mayoralty of Coyoacán is quite big, but you'll spend most of your time in Centro de Coyoacán. This charming area is known for its bohemian vibe and colourful houses. It's a must-visit thanks to its parks, its traditional market, Mercado Coyoacán (see p.205), and Museo Frida Kahlo (see p.149).

NUEVO POLANCO

This area mainly comprises three neighbourhoods: Granada, Ampliación Granada and Anáhuac, located north of Polanco. The area is growing very quickly thanks to the development of many office and residential buildings, as well as shopping malls like Antara Fashion Hall and Plaza Carso. You'll find two of the city's newer museums here: Museo Jumex (see p.175) and Museo Soumaya (see p.151).

SAN ÁNGEL

The origins of this lovely neighbourhood can be traced back to colonial times, when the Spanish founded Convento del Carmen, which is why there are quite a few religious buildings around here, like Iglesia San Jacinto (Plaza San Jacinto 18). Later on, during Porfirio Díaz's presidency during the 18th and 19th centuries, many rich families built their weekend homes here, giving the area its provincial feel. Today, it's a perfect escape for buying art and traditional crafts – don't miss a shopping spree at El Bazaar Sábado (see p.207), as well as exploring its varied culinary offerings, like the modern Mexican eatery Carlota (Plaza del Carmen 4).

XOCHIMILCO

Located in the southern part of the city, here's where you'll find the famous Xochimilco canals, originally built by the Aztecs as a water transportation system. It's a fascinating daytrip to board a trajinera boat to eat traditional food and listen to lively music; and there are companies and tour operators that will take you to see the chinamperos (the farmers who grow vegetables on the floating gardens) in action (see p.152).

NOTABLE NEIGHBOURHOODS

TABACALERA

Located in the centre of the city, this small neighbourhood is home to two important historic attractions: Monumento a la Revolución (MRM, see p.155), an impressive landmark that celebrates the Mexican Revolution that you can actually explore from its inside, and Museo Nacional de San Carlos (see p.157), home to an incredible collection of European art.

SAN RAFAEL

One of the oldest neighbourhoods in town, it boasts beautiful 19th-century mansions and is also home to several theatres. Over the past few years, it has become popular among a younger, artistic crowd, drawn to the area for its convenient location and affordable prices. Don't miss a visit to Galería Hilario Galguera (see p.181), known for its contemporary art offerings.

SAN MIGUEL CHAPULTEPEC

This peaceful neighbourhood is conveniently located right across Bosque de Chapultepec park (see p.10). It is mostly residential, but also features a few restaurants, galleries – like kurimanzutto (see p.183), a must-see for contemporary art lovers – and coffee shops, and is known for its beautiful, French-inspired homes.

SANTA FE

The city's business district has tall office buildings, luxury hotels, college campuses and several shopping malls. If you're in town for business and you're staying or working in this area, make time to check out Park Plaza shopping mall, home to Cañamiel concept store (see p.208) and Cascabel, a restaurant that serves traditional Mexican fare with a modern twist.

CIUDAD UNIVERSITARIA

Home to the main campus of UNAM (National Autonomous University of Mexico), the name of this neighbourhood literally translates to University City. Here, you'll find the university's museum of contemporary art: MUAC (see p.185), worth checking out both for its interesting temporary exhibitions and the modern building that houses it.

CLAVERÍA

Located in the northern part of the city, this neighbourhood is mostly residential, but locals and visitors alike know it's home to a beloved traditional restaurant, Nicos (see p.98).

LOMAS DE CHAPULTEPEC

This tranquil residential neighbourhood boasts tree-lined streets and a few restaurants and coffee shops, mostly populated by locals. It's quite close to Juárez and Polanco, and it is worth stopping for lunch or dinner at Carmela y Sal (see p.99), one of the most interesting restaurants to open in the city in recent years.

GUADALUPE INN

This southern neighbourhood has office buildings and private homes, but you'll find culinary treasures like the Provence-inspired Loretta Chic Bistrot (see p.101) and its sister restaurant, Eloise (Av. Revolución 1521).

PEDREGAL

This residential area, created as a modernist project in the '40s, has some of the prettiest private homes in the city, and is home to Sud 777 (see p.103), a top fine-dining destination. Recently, a luxury shopping mall, Artz Pedregal, was added to the landscape.

COLONIA DEL VALLE

What was once the Jesuit-run Hacienda de San Francisco de Borja, dedicated to raising horses, cows and goats in the 16th century, is now one of the largest neighbourhoods in the city. You'll find office buildings, private residences and businesses but the main reason to head there is to have an unforgettable breakfast at Fonda Margarita (see p.105).

JAMAICA

This neighbourhood located towards the centre of the city is home to many small retail businesses but the highlight is Mercado Jamaica (see p. 209), a sprawling market that sells hundreds of fresh flowers and plants.

ROMA NORTE/CONDESA

FULL-DAY ITINERARY

Bars, restaurants, art galleries, design stores … there is so much going on in these two neighbourhoods, home to a big part of the city's creative population, which, of course, has extended to many of the surrounding areas. Roma Norte and Condesa remain highly popular and fun to discover. Enjoy a day exploring their classic spots and their new offerings, with no rush at all.

10AM Fuel up with a strong cold brew and a warm chocolate babka at ① **Dosis Café** (see p.37), one of the coolest coffee houses in Roma Norte. Then, take Frontera and walk a couple of blocks north to Colima, where you'll find ② **PROYECTOSMONCLOVA**, (see p.167), a contemporary art gallery with an intriguing line-up of Mexican and international artists.

12PM When you leave the gallery, continue right along Colima and you'll reach ③ **Escópica** (see p.189), a family-run shop with a beautifully curated selection of eyewear and sunglasses and a lovely décor that is worth checking out. Afterwards, cross the street and find out what interesting exhibition is being held at the design-oriented ④ **Museo del Objeto del Objeto** (**MODO**, see p.165).

1.30PM Continue down Colima and turn right on Orizaba until you reach ⑤ **Plaza Río de Janeiro**, one of the prettiest parks in the city. Cross the plaza and you'll find your lunch spot, ⑥ **Sartoria** (see p.65), where an incredible Italian meal awaits. Across the street, you'll spot a colourful candy/lolly store called ⑦ **Dulcería de Celaya.** Head there after lunch and marvel at the dozens of traditional Mexican sweets available – they make for the perfect dessert. Don't skip their cocadas (coconut-and-milk treats) or puerquitos (brown sugar cookies shaped like pigs).

4PM It's time for a slightly longer walk. From the park, take Calle de Durango and walk along its tree-lined central division. This street will take you all the way to ⑧ **Fuente de Cibeles** (a replica of Madrid's own famous fountain, and one of Roma Norte's most action-packed areas), and then along the Plaza Villa de Madrid to Condesa when you make a left on Medellín. You'll find cute shops along the way, like ⑨ **Roma Quince Concept Store** (Medellín 67), stocked with beautiful home décor items, so take your time to explore.

5PM Make a right on Avenue Álvaro Obregón, and then a left on Calle Cacahuamilpa until you reach ⑩ **Avenida Amsterdam** which is, in my opinion, one of the prettiest streets in the whole city. Make a left on Amsterdam and you'll soon realise that it's a circuit – that's because it used to be a horse racing track – Condesa is actually called Hipódromo (Racecourse) Condesa, so if you're up for it, you can walk the whole loop. It's a lovely, tree-lined street, with many restaurants and coffee shops, but peaceful enough that you'll spot locals walking their pets or taking a nice stroll.

6PM When you reach the corner with Iztaccíhuatl, make a left across the plaza and pop into ⑪ **Baltra** (see p.123), an intimate cocktail bar with both original creations and excellent classics. I especially love the vodka martini and the Negroni here.

7PM After a drink or two, head back across the small plaza and along Iztaccíhuatl until you reach Avenida México, which you can choose to follow along to the right, or wander through Parque México and up Avenue Sonora towards ⑫ **Merkavá** (see p.85), where you can end your day with a fantastic Israeli feast. While the extensive menu might make it a bit hard to choose, the good news is that almost everything here is meant to be shared. Don't miss the salatim (a selection of traditional salads) and the chocolate babka French toast for the grand finale, paired with a cup of steaming Turkish coffee.

Itinerary

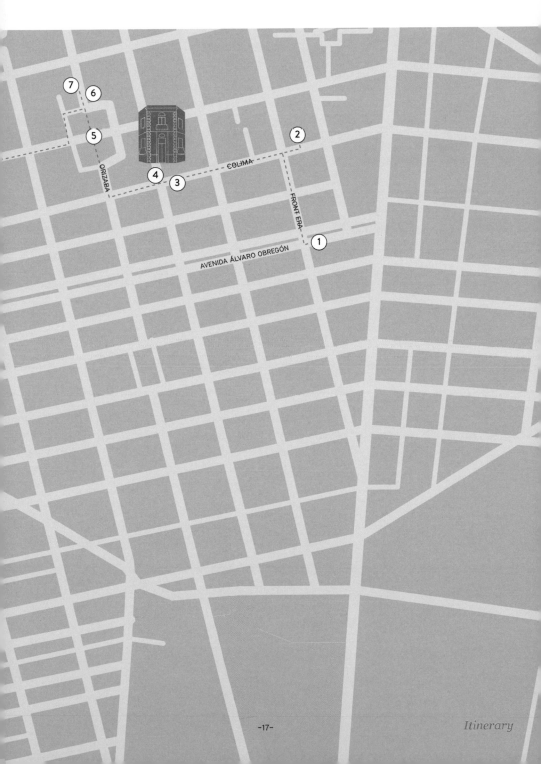

Itinerary

CENTRO HISTÓRICO
FULL-DAY ITINERARY

The name says it all: the city's historic downtown concentrates a great deal of its cultural offerings, found not only inside the many wonderful museums and historic sites but on the streets themselves. There are around 1500 historic buildings, including churches, parks, museums and fountains, making the area a UNESCO World Heritage Site since 1987. On this tour, you will also witness the city at its liveliest: the streets are busy, there's music playing and you'll get a history lesson with every step.

9AM If there's a classic spot to have breakfast in Mexico City, it has to be ① **El Cardenal** (see p.72), housed inside the Hilton Mexico City Reforma. Its legendary hot chocolate, sweet and foamy, paired with a hot-from-the-oven pastry, will give you the energy you need to head outside for a nice stroll through ② **Alameda Central**. This sprawling public park is the oldest in Mexico and all of the Americas (it was founded in 1592) and is decorated with several fountains and sculptures such as *Life and Peace* by Antonio Álvarez Portugal.

11AM Walk through the park towards the corner of Avenida Juárez and Eje Central, to the gorgeous ③ **Palacio de Bellas Artes** museum (see p.139). Admire its white marble facade and its Art Deco interior and linger for an interesting temporary exhibition. On your way out, look up and you'll spot the ④ **Torre Latinoamericana**, a 45-level skyscraper that was built by architect Augusto H. Álvarez and was the tallest building in the city until 1972, when the World Trade Center was built.

1PM From the Palacio de Bellas Artes, turn left on Eje Central, and then make a right on Tacuba, where you'll find ⑤ **Museo Nacional de Arte** (see p.133). This building by famed architect Manuel Tolsá holds an incredible collection of Mexican art, from the vice-regal period (from the 16th century to 1810) to the 1950s. Make sure you check out the gorgeous landscapes by Gerardo Murillo, best known as Dr. Atl. After a dose of culture, walk down Calle de Filomeno Mata and find ⑥ **La Ópera**, an old-school cantina where, according to legend, revolutionary hero Pancho Villa fired a bullet to the ceiling, just to show off during one of his visits in the early 19th century. Kick back with a shot of tequila and try their famous octopus a la gallega (with potatoes, red peppers, and olive oil).

3PM After lunch, take a slightly longer walk down Avenida Cinco de Mayo until you reach ⑦ **Zócalo** (see p.143), the city's main square. The sprawling plaza is surrounded by important buildings: **Catedral Metropolitana**, the city cathedral; **Palacio Nacional**, the seat of the federal executive; and **Museo del Templo Mayor** (see p.135), a major archaeological site of a 14th century temple of the Mexica peoples. You'll be impressed at how this area concentrates so much of the country's long and rich history: you can walk from a pre-Hispanic construction to a Baroque cathedral in a matter of minutes.

5.30PM Walk back towards Avenida Cinco de Mayo and head up to ⑧ **El Balcón del Zócalo** for a drink and a few appetisers. This restaurant has an excellent view of the square, so it will give you a front row seat to the flag-lowering ceremony, which takes place every evening at 6pm.

8PM Time for dinner! Head back along Avenida Cinco de Mayo and turn right when you reach Calle de Bolívar. Continue walking until you reach Ignacio Allende, where you'll find ⑨ **Limosneros** (see p. 73) on your right. Here, you'll find a traditional Mexican menu with modern touches, plus plenty of opportunities to try insect-based dishes – ask the staff for suggestions. The restaurant also offers tasty cocktails and a fascinating variety of national spirits, from mezcal (made from agave) to pox (a corn-based drink from the state of Chiapas). To toast like a local, say 'salud!' while looking at the person directly in the eye – otherwise it's bad luck!

10PM If the drinks at Limosneros get you in the mood to explore this world a little further, head over to ⑩ **Bósforo** (see p.119) on Luis Moya (it's probably late by now, so I suggest an Uber or a cab that the restaurant can call for you). The entrance to this non-descript bar might fool you, but it's the perfect place to try several kinds of mezcal, thanks to its low-key vibe and helpful expert staff.

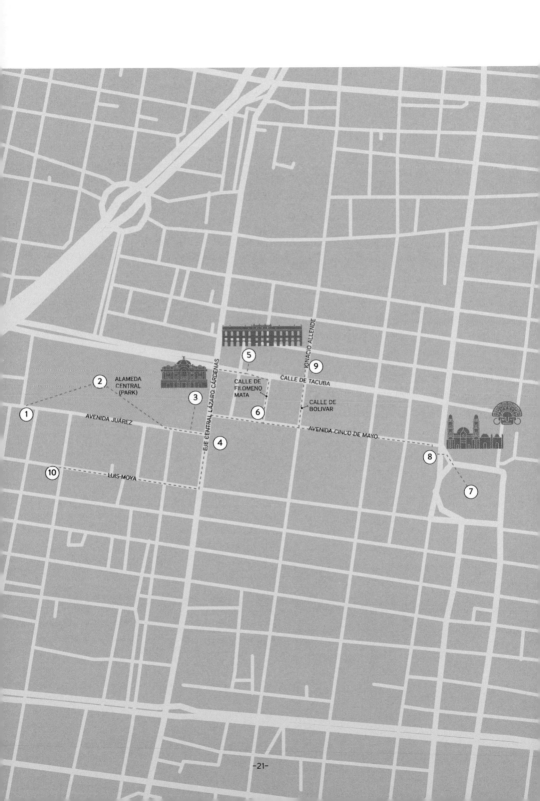

ALAMEDA
CENTRAL
(PARK)

AVENIDA JUÁREZ

EJE CENTRAL LÁZARO CÁRDENAS

CALLE DE
FILOMENO
MATA

IGNACIO ALLENDE

CALLE DE TACUBA

CALLE DE
BOLIVAR

AVENIDA CINCO DE MAYO

LUIS MOYA

1
2
3
4
5
6
7
8
9
10

JUÁREZ/REFORMA
HALF-DAY ITINERARY

Paseo de la Reforma is the city's main avenue, and it runs all the way from Centro Histórico to the business district of Santa Fe. Many of the most important museums, monuments and luxury hotels, as well as the tallest skyscrapers, have been built along Reforma, and its sidewalks/footpaths are a sort of open-air museum. You will always find an art exhibition to enjoy while you walk, plus a healthy dose of folklore – be it a live music performance, a crafts vendor or a street-food cart.

12PM Surrounded by the Bosque de Chapultepec park, ⓵ **Museo Tamayo** (see p.173) is one of the city's hotspots for modern and contemporary art, and it never fails to offer fascinating temporary exhibitions. Oaxacan painter Rufino Tamayo, one of Mexico's most celebrated artists, started this museum in 1981. Start your afternoon here – as it tends to get a bit crowded – and then take Calzada Mahatma Gandhi and turn left onto Paseo de la Reforma, which will literally lead you out of the woods.

1PM As you walk down Paseo de la Reforma, you'll see some of the skyscrapers that have transformed the city's landscapes over the past few

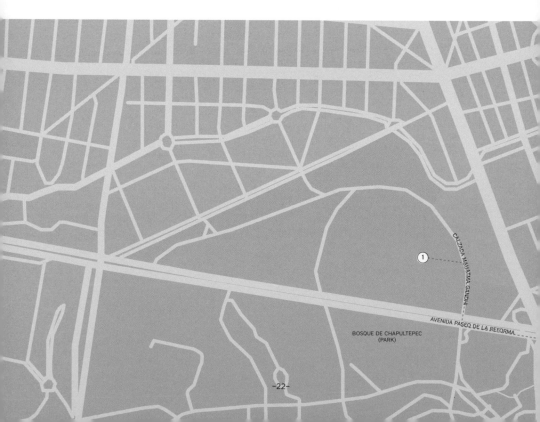

years. To your right, there is ② **Torre Bancomer,** with 53 floors; and to your left, ③ **Torre Mayor**, with 59 floors, and the impressive ④ **Torre Reforma**, which has been placed atop a 20th-century mansion. Continuing up Paseo de la Reforma you'll also spot important landmarks, like ⑤ **Fuente de la Diana Cazadora**, followed by the iconic ⑥ **Ángel de la Independencia**, the 45-metre (147-foot) victory column that watches over the avenue. The angel was built by architect Antonio Díaz Mercado in 1910, when Porfirio Díaz was president, and though it suffered some damage in the 1957 earthquake, it has stood proudly ever since.

2PM When you reach the roundabout of Glorieta de la Palma, turn right on Niza, then left on Londres, and right again on Havre. There, you'll find ⑦ **Havre 77** (see p.83), chef Eduardo García's delicious brasserie. A platter of fresh oysters and a glass of champagne will help you recover some of the calories you just burned on your walk.

4PM After this late lunch, cross the street and head over to ⑧ **Casa Caballería** (see p.197), a carefully curated store for men, with tailor-made jeans and fancy grooming products. And if you need some caffeine, chef Elena Reygadas' cosy ⑨ **Café Nin** (see p.81) offers great coffee and pastries.

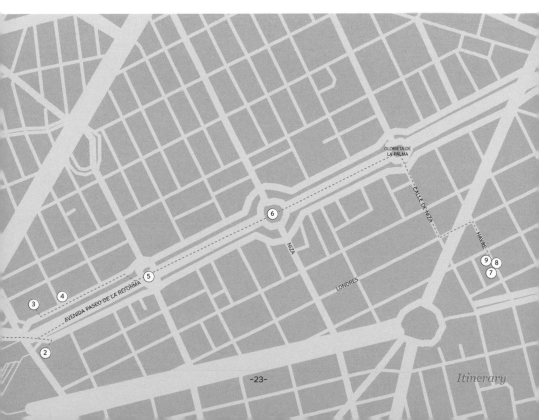

Itinerary

COYOACÁN

FULL-DAY ITINERARY

Located in the southern part of the city, Coyoacán is full of charm and culture. With its cobblestone streets and cheerful plazas, it sometimes feels like it's not really a part of the city, but perhaps a smaller town, where time runs a little bit slower. Find souvenirs at the market, learn all about Frida Kahlo at her house-turned-museum, and treat yourself to all sorts of delicious snacks from street vendors, like hot churros and creamy esquites.

11AM Start your day with some culture and colour at ① **Museo Frida Kahlo** (see p.149), also known as La Casa Azul. The house Kahlo shared with husband Diego Rivera has been turned into a museum that honours her work and her spirit. It's wise to buy tickets in advance through the museum website, as this is an immensely popular attraction.

1PM Walk down Ignacio Allende until you reach ② **Mercado Coyoacán** (see p.205), and get lost among stalls and stalls of fruits and vegetables, traditional crafts, colourful piñatas, and candles and herbs. If you get hungry, the amazing tostadas (crispy corn tortillas topped with chicken, meat, shrimp, and other delicious options), at the very centre of the market, will keep you energised until you sit down for a full meal later in the day.

3PM Continue your path along Ignacio Allende and you'll find ③ **Jardín Hidalgo**, one of the most popular squares in town, where you can admire the ④ **San Juan Bautista** church and convent and the French-style gazebo.

5PM Walk over to the lovely Jardín Centenario, and have a seat at ⑤ **Los Danzantes** (see p.96), where your Oaxacan-inspired meal will be paired with an excellent selection of mezcal. Afterwards, wander back across the lively square, populated by balloon vendors, fortune-tellers, and all sorts of colourful characters.

7PM End your day with a cup of coffee – or a creative coffee-based cocktail – at ⑥ **Café Avellaneda** (see p.51), which you'll find if you stroll along Higuera for a few minutes. This cosy coffee shop is a favourite among locals from the neighbourhood and beyond for its top-notch beans and low-key atmosphere.

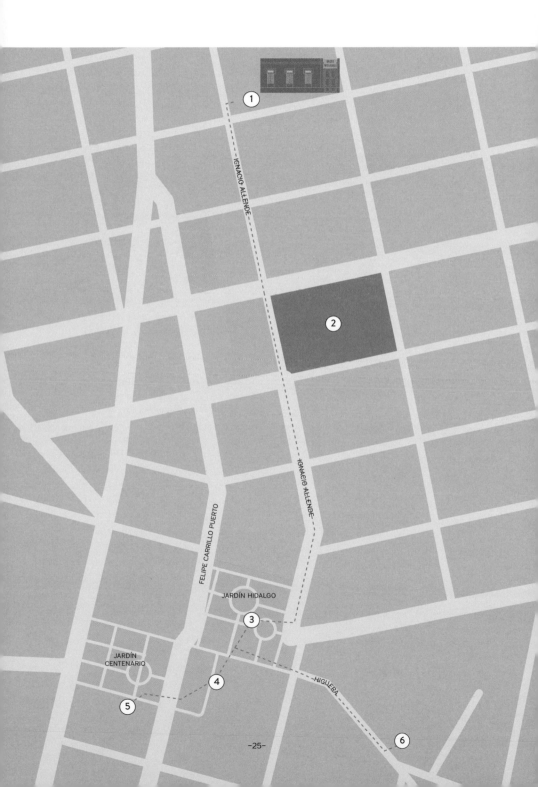

POLANCO
HALF-DAY ITINERARY

The poshest neighbourhood in the city is perfect for a relaxing day of shopping. You'll find pretty much every designer name you want, as well as some of the top-rated restaurants in town. Bring a comfortable pair of shoes and get ready to treat yourself.

10AM Avenida Presidente Masaryk is home to an incredible selection of luxury boutiques, but before you start your shopping spree, get a hearty breakfast at ① **Guzina Oaxaca** (Presidente Masaryk 513), run by famed chef Alejandro Ruiz. His Oaxacan specialties (including tamales and enchiladas) will energise you to explore boutiques like Dolce & Gabbana, Salvatore Ferragamo and Louis Vuitton. Keep your eyes open for Mexican brands like Lorena Saravia (Presidente Masaryk and Tennyson), known for her contemporary designs for women, and TANE (Presidente Masaryk 430), a classic silversmith firm, famous for their jewellery and home decoration pieces.

PARQUE
LINCOLN

2PM Shopping takes a lot of energy, so when you reach Aristóteles, turn right and head over to ② **Parque Lincoln**. This lovely park is surrounded by lively restaurants, cafes and bars, so you have plenty of options. There are Italian, Japanese, seafood, and French restaurants, so it's really up to your cravings. But if you want a privileged view of the park, you can't go wrong with ③ **Emilio** (Emilio Castelar 107), which serves a varied, international menu. Their pork belly tacos are a highlight.

4PM After lunch, you can have a potent espresso at ④ **Joselo** (see p.49), also on Emilio Castelar, or perhaps turn right on Julio Verne for a warm churro at ⑤ **El Moro**, one of many around town (see p.80). Walk around the park and let the afternoon go slowly by.

XOCHIMILCO

HALF-DAY ITINERARY

Though it takes a bit of time to get to the floating gardens of Xochimilco, they are unlike anything else you'll see in the city, so they're worth making time for. Keep in mind that this is not a walking itinerary, so you'll need a car, taxi or ride-share. You can stop at Museo Dolores Olmedo on your way back if you want to add some more culture to the journey, or spend the entire day relaxing along the canals, surrounded by colourful trajineras (traditional wooden boats) offering food and live music.

10AM Arrive at ① **Embarcadero Nativitas** and board a colorful trajinera boat, which will take you to explore the canals of **Xochimilco** (see p.152). During your tour, you'll spot many trajineras offering tacos, esquites, and all kinds of treats, while others carry mariachi bands and marimba players to liven up your tour. If you want to see the work of the chinamperos (the farmers who grow vegetables on the floating gardens) up close, you can contact **Yolcan** (yolcan.com). This organisation promotes sustainable agriculture and connects chinampa farmers with local consumers and chefs and offers two different tours, leaving from Embarcadero Cuemanco.

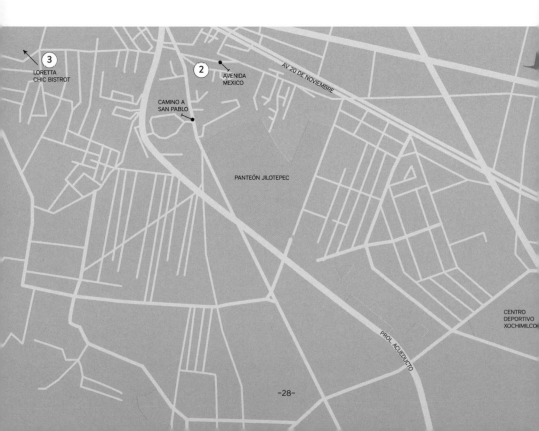

2PM It will take you about 20 minutes by car to get from Embarcadero Nativitas to ② **Museo Dolores Olmedo** (see p.153), housed in a beautiful 16th-century hacienda (an estate built in colonial times) called La Noria. Here, you'll find the largest Diego Rivera and Frida Kahlo collection in the country (including Frida's iconic *Self-portrait with Monkey*), as well as peaceful gardens populated by friendly hairless dogs called xoloitzcuintles.

4PM If you're hungry after the museum and you're headed back to the central area of the city, you can stop at Guadalupe Inn at ③ **Loretta Chic Bistrot** (see p.101) for a late lunch. It will take you half an hour to get there by car. This lovely restaurant serves a Mediterranean-inspired menu and offers an excellent selection of wines.

CARRETERA FEDERAL 113

CALLE DEL MERCADO ①

Itinerary

COFFEE

Among the countless great foods that are produced in Mexico, I have to mention coffee. The green, foggy states of Chiapas, Veracruz and Oaxaca are among the world's top coffee-growing regions, and while producers have been working the land for hundreds of years, it seems like the rest of us weren't paying enough attention. While there are honourable mentions included in this chapter   places with long histories, like Café Villarías (see p. 39) and Tierra Garat (see p. 45) – there weren't, until recently, enough places that gave Mexican coffee the platform it deserves.

Fortunately, there are now plenty of great spots that honour this national treasure, from small spots with super-focused menus, like Buna (see p. 38), to larger chains, like Cielito Querido (see p. 48). But it's not all about keeping things strictly local. Places like Quentin (see p. 35) and Almanegra Café (see p. 33) serve coffee produced overseas, as long as it's excellent and worth sharing. And after all, isn't that what we all want from a cup of coffee?

Almanegra Café

*Specialty coffee and gourmet pastries
in a sleek space.*

This story began in 2014, when a trio of friends – Octavio, Matzuko and Gabriel – decided to team up and bring a top-notch coffee house to their neighbourhood, Colonia Narvarte. A couple of years later, they opened a second, larger location, here in Roma Norte, where the goal remains the same: to serve the cleanest, most balanced specialty coffee – only beans that score 80 points or higher make it to Almanegra. Beans can come from Mexican regions, like Oaxaca and Chiapas, or other countries, and a seasonal rotation means that you'll always find three options: a washed coffee, a natural coffee and a guest coffee (previous collaborations include roasters from Berlin and Colorado).

    Straightforward drinks are the best way to understand the Almanegra approach. Try the cappuccino or the cold-brew nitro (which you can take with you in a beautiful, recyclable bottle) or the Gibraltar, like a flat white–style served in a 'Gibraltar glass' that pays tribute to San Francisco's legendary Blue Bottle coffee. If you love carbs, you'll find joy in the cookies provided by Kim's Kitchen (in flavours like s'mores and lavender), and in the pastries baked by fellow Narvarte baker, Panadería Costra, like the three-chocolate concha (sweet bread) and the caramelised banana and chocolate tart.

Tonalá 53, Roma Norte

Niños Héroes, line 3
Jardín Pushkin, line 3

Mon–Sun 8am–9pm

$MXN

$34–$80

W

almanegracafe.mx

Coffee

Quentin

Coffee that is cared for from bean to cup.

Coffee is serious business at this cosy Roma Norte spot. Founder Menachem Gancz found the inspiration for the project after a trip to Chiapas, one of Mexico's main coffee-producing states. With top quality in mind, he and his team have developed sustainable relationships with small producers who hail both from Mexico and other countries, like Honduras, Kenya and Ethiopia, making sure that the coffee source is known and the beans are cared for throughout the entire process. Once the beans arrive in town, they are roasted in-house and used to prepare cup after excellent cup.

Head to the marble bar, where the team of baristas is ready to answer any question you may have regarding flavour, origins or preparation methods and equally eager to suggest something if you're not quite sure what to get. There's no going wrong with their espresso or excellent flat white–style but there are also a couple of interesting house specialties that are definitely worth a try. They serve a refreshing cascara iced tea, made with the dried skins of coffee cherries, and a delicious carajillo – a mix of espresso and Licor 43, a sweet digestive liquor; both are perfect at one of the footpath (sidewalk) tables during a warm afternoon.

Álvaro Obregón 64,
Roma Norte

Sun–Wed 8am–10pm
Thurs–Sat 8am–11pm

$MXN
$40–$70

Niños Héroes, line 3
Jardín Pushkin, line 3

Dosis Café

*Chill out and enjoy Mexican coffee and great
breakfasts at this cafe and cultural space.*

Long wooden benches and a varied, eclectic playlist set the mood at this hip coffee shop right from the moment you step in. Its founders brought their expertise home after working in cafes in San Francisco and opened here in 2015. With beans from Veracruz, Chiapas and Oaxaca, there's excellent cappuccinos and espressos but their cold brew is also a winner. Frequent clients are also fans of the hot chocolate, a lovely DIY treat: get the hot milk and melt the block of chocolate in it.

If you're here for breakfast, have the hearty toasts, served on homemade sourdough bread and topped with ingredients like avocado, eggs, Nutella or almond butter. The chocolate babka and the chunky chocolate chip cookie are delicious, too. And if you're in the mood for something stronger than coffee, you can order a glass of wine or a nice cold beer.

Aside from being a coffee shop, Dosis also functions as a cultural forum, hosting yoga lessons, meditation sessions or music performances from time to time.

Álvaro Obregón 24B,
Roma Norte

Niños Héroes, line 3
Jardín Pushkin, line 3

Mon–Fri 9am–9pm
Sat 10am–9pm
Sun 11am–9pm

$MXN
$40–$90

W
dosiscafe.com

Coffee

Buna

A cute little shop with a simple mission: to serve great Mexican coffee.

Orizaba 42, Roma

Niños Héroes, line 3
Jardín Pushkin, line 3

Mon–Thurs 8am–7pm
Fri–Sat 8am–10pm

$MXN

$40 per cup

W

buna.mx

Its great location, right off the lovely Plaza Río de Janeiro, and its outdoor tables, make Buna perfect for people-watching. And it serves truly good coffee, reflecting the motto: cafe rico. You can choose from a selection of 10 drinks, from espresso to house creation, the cafechata – cold brew with horchata (particularly good on a warm day). The drinks are complemented by fluffy pastries baked fresh by their neighbours, the excellent Italian restaurant, Sartoria (see p.65).

The Buna team spends several months a year exploring Mexico's coffee-growing regions, and establishing relationships with producers. You can taste the results here and by purchasing the beans.

Café Villarías

Coffee roasters with a fascinating history.

López 68-A, Centro

Salto del Agua, lines 1, 8
Plaza San Juan, line 4

Mon–Sat 9am–6.45pm

$MXN

$50

W

cafevillarias.com

The smell of freshly roasted coffee will lead coffee aficionados here. The Villarías family business started as a fish cannery in Spain, in 1897, with three sardines as its logo. When the civil war started, the family fled to France, staying until World War II, then moved to Mexico. Here, they traded fish for coffee, hence why the logo is now three coffee beans.

The family's mission continues – to sell the highest quality Mexican coffee. Grown at more than 1200 metres (3937 feet) above sea level in Chiapas, they roast caracolillo and planchuela beans – both from the arabica family. While you can't try it here, it's definitely worth visiting so the well-informed staff can advise you on roasting and preparing coffee at home.

Chiquitito Café

Small in size but big on heart.

A favourite among locals in Condesa, tiny Chiquitito Café (literal translation for little coffee shop) was born in 2012 to offer the best possible cup of coffee in the cosiest atmosphere. To achieve this, the team works with Mexican coffee growers – particularly Carlos Avendaño from Boca del Río, Veracruz, one of the most important coffee-producing regions in Mexico – making sure that the beans are traced throughout the process and up until the moment they reach the cup.

The professionals behind the bar are ready to tell you about the available methods, including aero press, pour-over, Chemex and French press, and also make you an excellent iced espresso. If a cup of java is not your thing, you can go for a matcha or a nice chai latte. If you're hungry, go for the PB&J sandwich, the bagel with cream cheese or the avocado toast with fetta. And if you have extra room in your suitcase, make sure you take a bag of coffee beans with you.

Chiquitito has two more locations: in Cuauhtémoc (Río Lerma 179) and in Lomas de Chapultepec (Prado Norte 421A).

Alfonso Reyes 232 E,
Condesa

Chilpancingo, line 9
Chilpancingo, line 1

Mon–Sat
7.30am–8.30pm
Sun 9am–6.30pm

$MXN

$60–$100

W

chiquititocafe.com

Coffee

Blend Station

*A friendly local space
to work or chat.*

Tamaulipas 60, Condesa

Chilpancingo, line 9
Chilpancingo, line 1

Mon–Sat 7am–10pm
Sun 8am–10pm

$MXN

$50–$100

W

blendstation.com.mx

This is one of the most welcoming spaces
in Condesa, with illustrations lining the walls,
a large tree growing in the middle of the
room and a skylight making the room bright
and airy. It's a favourite among students
and freelancers.

Mexican coffee is the star of the
show here, thanks to founder Alejandro
Fortes and his dream of promoting local
beans – his team works with an agricultural
engineer and a chemist to help coffee
producers improve their crops. You can
also try non-coffee creations, such as a
matcha latte or fizzy homemade sodas –
the violet-flavoured one is really good. The
huge cookies go well with your drink and
there are sandwiches, toasts and muffins,
all baked in-house.

Café Budapest Cukraszda

This adorable spot is a love letter to Hungary and its desserts.

Tamaulipas 130, Condesa

Chilpancingo, line 9
Chilpancingo, line 1

Mon–Sat 11am–10pm
Sun 11am–8pm

$MXN

$40–$120

This incredibly charming coffee house, owned by Gabriela Biringer, is a tribute to her Hungarian heritage, which you will find in every detail: pictures of the Hungarian parliament and of her family, traditional tea sets, classical music and quirky details, like the table with an antique sink and the colourful plates on the exterior.

Gabriela bakes Hungarian desserts from original recipes, like black forest cake, and her specialty – the sacher torte, prepared with chocolate, nutmeg, and apricot jam. Pair it with a strong Turkish coffee, or for something less strong, try the tea selection. The food menu also features savoury options, including empanadas, bagels and crepes.

Tierra Garat

Mexican coffee and chocolate are the stars here.

With its warm, earthy tones and details of wood and leather, this coffee and cocoa shop evokes the feeling of a Mexican ranch, with a contemporary twist. The carefully designed interiors of this spot (and the other 17 locations across town) are the work of prestigious Mexican designers, Héctor Esrawe and Ignacio Cadena, who were commissioned to build a home for Café Garat, the brand that established itself a couple of decades ago as the first gourmet coffee to be sold in Mexican supermarkets.

The menu is quite extensive, as it focuses both on Mexican coffee and cocoa, two of our great treasures. There are traditional coffee-based drinks (espresso, cortado), cocoa options (like the Negra Flor, with vanilla, or the Criollo, with natural cocoa), or coffee-and-cocoa combos. Additionally, you can pick from a selection of herbal tea and fruit infusions (I love the iced version of the kiwi–passionfruit tea), as well as frappé drinks, like chai and taro. On the food front, you'll find pastries and sandwiches, healthy snacks, like quinoa bars, and the especially popular tarts (try the guava). And if you want to take a little something as a keepsake, check out the shelves for pottery, fruit jams and artisanal soaps.

Nuevo León 122, Condesa

Chilpancingo, line 9
Chilpancingo, line 1

Mon–Sat 7am–10pm
Sun 8am–10pm

$MXN

$30–$65

W

tierragarat.mx

Tomás

Explore the world of tea at this welcoming space.

As a special exception, we've included a tea house in this chapter. Visiting Tomás is an easy and fun way to delve into the world of tea, even for those who know very little about it. The dozens of numbered tins behind the counter shouldn't intimidate you, as the knowledgeable staff members are ready to guide you along your journey. Ask about the types of teas and tisanes available, such as white, green, mate and oolong, and the specialised blends that you can only find here. They'll love to answer your questions.

The options are endless and you can smell as many teas as you want until you find your favourite. Next, it's time to decide the best way to drink it – whether it's hot, cold or frappé; sweetened or unsweetened; with or without milk. Within a few minutes, you'll have a totally customised tea in your hands. Not just that, you'll learn the benefits of it. The Maison de Canelle, for example, is a sweet blend of apples, almonds, cinnamon and beets that helps your cardiovascular system and tastes great as a frappé drink. Head to one of the comfortable couches inside or pick a footpath (sidewalk) table and watch the afternoon go by.

Tamaulipas 66, Condesa

Chilpancingo, line 9
Chilpancingo, line 1

Mon–Fri 8am–10pm
Sat–Sun 9am–10pm

$MXN
$70–$85

W

tomas.mx

Coffee

Cielito Querido

*A colourful celebration
of Mexican flavours.*

Masaryk 29, Polanco

Polanco, line 7

Mon–Fri 7am–10pm
Sat–Sun 8am–10pm

$MXN

$35–$75

W

cielitoquerido.com.mx

Packed with a playful personality, Cielito burst onto the city's coffee scene in 2010, as a local alternative to the international chains. Today, there are more than 100 locations in Mexico City. With mismatched chairs and sofas, pretty tiled floors, clever messages on the walls and decorated napkins and coffee cups, Cielito celebrates all things Mexican.

You'll find cappuccinos and lattes but the true stars are Mexican-inspired concoctions, like the deliciously refreshing chamoyadas – iced drinks in flavours like lime, mango, and tangerine, with hot chamoy syrup, and many twists on the horchata. There are also hearty sandwiches and pastries that showcase local flavours, like cornbread and sweet conchas.

Joselo

Excellent espresso in the cafe or take-away in the park.

Emilio Castelar 107, Polanco

Polanco, line 7

Mon–Fri 7am–9.45pm
Sat–Sun 8am–9pm

$MXN

$40–$80

Located right in front of Parque Lincoln, this coffee shop buzzes from morning to evening with locals. Many of them would probably say they're here for the espresso, although the baristas are particularly proud of their cappuccino, which they prepare Italian-style (and yes, it deserves the praise). To achieve coffee greatness, beans are from the renowned producing region of Jaltenango, Chiapas, and roasted in-house.

You'll find simple, satisfying food, like bagels, fruit bowls, pastries and cookies. If the fig croissant is available, don't let it pass you by. Snag a footpath (sidewalk) table, or if it's too crowded, take your drink and walk around the park.

Coffee

Café Negro

*Fresh-baked bread
and Mexican coffee
in a laid-back space.*

———————————————

Centenario 16, Coyoacán

Mon–Sun 8am–11pm

$MXN

$30–$60

W

cafenegrocoyoacan.com

This is one of the friendliest spots in Coyoacán and one of the busiest, too, as it is located just steps away from the popular Jardín Centenario. You're bound to find groups of friends, couples and freelancers with their laptops, all drawn by the good drinks and pastries.

Café Negro proudly serves 100% Mexican coffee, from Guerrero, Chiapas, Oaxaca and Veracruz. Menu highlights include their espresso, mocha, flat white–style coffee, iced matcha and chai latte. The fresh-baked goods are brag-worthy: the chocolatín (chocolate croissant) and cinnamon rolls are super indulgent, as are the pies and tarts. If you're craving something savoury, there are pressed panini and delicious sandwiches on fresh ciabatta.

Café Avellaneda

Top-notch coffee and fun drinks in the heart of Coyoacán.

Higuera 40-A, Coyoacán

Mon–Fri 8am–10pm
Sat–Sun 10am–10pm

$MXN

$45–$80

Just a few steps from the Coyoacán market, this tiny nook pours some of the most interesting coffee in the city. There are just a few seats and some stools at the bar, but the choice of beans from regions like Chiapas, Veracruz and Oaxaca, and the friendly baristas helping you decide the best preparation method, like aero press, V60, or cold brew, will make you want to stay.

Have an espresso or a cortado but try a fun house specialty, like the Juanito: a fresh mix of espresso, tonic water, tamarind and juniper. Or the sweet Camelia, made with milk, maple, espresso and black tea. For a sweet tooth, brownies and loaves are pure comfort.

RESTAURANTS

With centuries-old culinary traditions and a complex range of ingredients – be ready to try different kinds of corn, aromatic herbs, chillies and even insects – it's no wonder that Mexican food is such an important part of our identity and was declared 'Intangible Cultural Heritage' by UNESCO in 2010.

But that's just part of the reason that eating here is such an exciting experience: it's not all about Mexican food. You can find authentic expressions of Japanese and Israeli cuisine, such as Rokai (see p.95) and Merkavá (see p.85), respectively; indulge in the most delightful comfort food at Niddo (see p.77); enjoy fresh seafood and farm-to-table concepts, too – see Contramar (see p.55) and Meroma (see p.61). And you'll encounter a dizzying variety of street food (see p.106). While neighbourhoods like Roma Norte, Condesa and Polanco offer some of the newest concepts, you're sure to find something delicious no matter what part of the city you're in.

Contramar

Great seafood and people-watching make
this Roma spot a must-visit.

Mexico City might be a few hours away from the beach, but a little more than 20 years ago, chef Gabriela Cámara decided to pretend like this wasn't true. By opening a seafood restaurant in Roma Norte, she gave people in the city a place in which to enjoy fresh fish in a laid-back environment, and helped kickstart the neighbourhood's transformation. To this day, Contramar's popularity hasn't waned one bit, so get there early for lunch or make a reservation a few weeks in advance.

So, what's all the fuss about? A menu built on the freshest fish and seafood available, featuring aguachiles (shrimp, lime juice, fresh chillies, sliced onions and cucumbers), seafood cocktails and al pastor fish tacos, among other delicacies. But if you want to go for the classics, take note: tuna tostadas (with avocado, mayonnaise and chipotle), pescado a la talla (a gorgeous grilled red snapper; half of it slathered in red chilli sauce, half in parsley sauce), and for the grand finale: the strawberry and meringue cake. Order a couple of carajillos (a mix of espresso and Licor 43) and let the afternoon become the evening. You will have then mastered the Mexican art of the sobremesa: lingering at the table after a great meal, no rush at all.

Durango 200,
Roma Norte

Sevilla, line 1
Durango, line 1

Sun–Thurs
12pm–6.30pm
Fri–Sat 12pm–8pm

$MXN

$145–$400

W

contramar.com.mx

La Docena

This import conquered the city, thanks to excellent ingredients and a lively scene.

Álvaro Obregón 31, Roma Norte

Niños Héroes, line 3
Jardín Pushkin, line 3

Mon–Sat 1.30pm–2.30am
Sun 1.30–11pm

$MXN

$150–$600

W

ladocena.com.mx

The craze for this oyster bar and grill started in Guadalajara – another Mexican city with a fantastic food scene – in 2012, and it wasn't long before chef Tomás Bermúdez and his team brought it to this neighbourhood of Mexico City.

Bermúdez believes that when you have top-quality product, you let the flavour shine through, so he skips the fussy preparations on the fish and seafood (flown in daily from the cold Pacific waters), produce (hailing from ranches in Jalisco, Xochimilco and Mexico City) and beef. The result: shareable trays of fresh oysters, bright ceviches and grilled meat cuts (and an awesome burger topped with Menonita cheese), which combined with the friendly service and an extensive drinks menu, make it the kind of place where lunch turns into afternoon drinks.

Promoting Mexican wine is also a priority here and La Docena even has its own labels, produced by Viñas de Garza in Baja California.

Rosetta

*Chef Elena Reygadas
serves creative dishes in
a romantic old house.*

Colima 166, Roma Norte

Sevilla, line 1
Durango, line 1

Mon–Sat 1.30–11.30pm

$MXN

$150–$540

W

rosetta.com.mx

There's something about this restaurant that feels like coming home. Perhaps it's because it is housed in a lovely old mansion, with high ceilings and flowery wallpaper. You'll feel as though chef Elena Reygadas herself has invited you over for lunch or dinner.

When it first opened back in 2011, Rosetta had a distinctly Italian soul that spoke of the time that Reygadas spent in Italian restaurants in London, but the menu has evolved, showing a chef who is willing to experiment without losing the flavours. The pastas are still fantastic and so is the bread, and the restaurant now has three of its own bakeries: Panadería Rosetta, in the city. But the constantly changing menu, ruled by seasonality, features more daring dishes, like a white mole (a complex sauce) with roasted carrots, and a dessert of rosemary ice-cream with fresh herbs and olive oil.

With its atmosphere, and attentive service, Rosetta proves that it has grown up, yet still feels like home.

Campobaja

A relaxed eatery serving fresh and seasonal
flavours from Baja California.

There's a Mexican saying that goes 'en el mar, la vida es más sabrosa', which roughly translates to: 'life is more delicious by the sea', and this easy, breezy spot is the place to prove it. The fresh flavours of the Baja California fields and waters are the main attraction, and chef Ezequiel Hernández, a Baja import himself, handles the ingredients with utmost care. He's also a firm advocate for responsible fishing, educating customers to eat only what the sea provides.

As such, seasonality and availability dictate the menu, and you might find creations like a San Quentin oyster with red uni, ponzu, olive oil and roe, or a cactus tostada topped with snapper and red clam ceviche. For the satisfying burritos, the flour tortillas are also flown in from the north.

Dishes like these taste even better when paired with a cold beer, and it's no surprise that Campobaja is a favourite for long weekend lunches, and especially for treating yourself after a night of one too many cocktails. The bright and airy room, outfitted with long wooden tables, rustic decor and a carefree vibe, will make you feel like you are, in fact, by the sea, even if it's just for a few hours.

Colima 124E, Roma Norte

Tues–Sat 1–6pm
Sun 1–7pm

$MXN

$100–$300

Cuauhtémoc, line 1
Jardín Pushkin, line 3

W

campobaja.com

Lalo

Breakfast and lunch are a casual yet delicious affair at this cheerful spot.

Zacatecas 173, Roma Norte

Hospital General, line 3
Jardín Pushkin, line 3

Tues–Sun 8am–6pm

$MXN

$200–$300

W

eat-lalo.com

The first sign that you're in for a treat is the colourful mural in the dining room, created by Belgian artist Dave Derop, a.k.a. Bué the Warrior. Here, chef Eduardo García – whose excellent Máximo Bistrot Local is right across the street – shows his casual, playful side, as seen in the restaurant's name (Lalo is short for Eduardo) and the long communal table where you can mingle with other guests as you eat.

García uses fresh, organic ingredients, and both breakfast and lunch options range from light and healthy to super indulgent. Start off your day with a flat white–style coffee and a plate of huevos con huitlacoche (fried eggs with corn mushroom, a local delicacy) or the legendary brioche French toast, served with mascarpone cheese and berries. At lunchtime, you can't go wrong with the wood-oven pizza but there are also lovely salads and pastas. Craft beers and house-made sodas make for perfect pairings.

Meroma

Unpretentious and delicious locally produced fare in a beautiful dining room.

Colima 150, Roma Norte

Niños Héroes, line 3
Jardín Pushkin, line 3

Tues–Sat 1.30–11pm
Sun 1.30–6pm

$MXN

$150–$350

W

meroma.mx

You'll fall in love with this restaurant, starting with the small bar at street level, where you can have a well-prepared cocktail before heading upstairs to one of the loveliest spaces in the city: all white walls and retro nods, like large mirrors and 1950s inspired chairs and banquettes, by Oficina de Práctica Arquitectónica studio. Chefs Rodney Cusic and Mercedes Bernal made their dream a reality and opened their own place in 2016 after working in major cities like New York and London.

The market-driven menu, in collaboration with small producers from the city and its surroundings, changes frequently, but bright and clever flavours are always to be found. House favourites, like a crudo made with the catch of the day, fried parsley, serrano chile and lemon vinaigrette, and the comforting orecchiette with lamb, smoked chillies, roasted broccoli and cheese, are great examples of the duo's skills and creativity. Leave room for the goat cheese tart – you won't regret it.

Reservations are recommended.

Fonda Fina

*Traditional Mexican cuisine with a clever twist
in a prime Roma spot.*

The friendly atmosphere and the charismatic chef – Juan Cabrera, who splits his time between Mexico City and Tijuana – are part of the reason that people keep coming back to this Mexican eatery. Perhaps the cheeky name is a factor, too. Fondas are super-casual places that serve full lunches, usually family run, and this 'fine fonda' makes it a point to keep things low key, even when the traditional food boasts a slightly sophisticated take.

Mexican wines and craft beers, as well as kitschy-cool cocktails, like the Negrito (whiskey, orange juice, fig and macerated mint leaves), will help you get settled as you browse through the menu, where you can build your own entrée (a protein with your sauce and side of choice), or choose among creations like the beautifully presented mushroom tamal with salsa borracha and spicy adobo. While Cabrera offers plenty of seasonal specials, fans would never forgive him if he removed certain classics from the menu, like the indulgent fideo seco (thin noodles cooked in tomato sauce) topped with green chilaquiles.

The restaurant's location – a few steps off Fuente de Cibeles – is yet another reason for its popularity and you'll be surrounded by a nice mix of families, businesspeople and Roma locals.

Medellín 79, Roma Norte

Mon–Wed 1–11pm
Thurs–Sat 1pm–12am
Sun 1–7pm

$MXN

$150–$250

Sevilla, line 1
Durango, line 1

W

fondafina.com.mx

Sartoria

Homemade pastas, excellent antipasti and a welcoming atmosphere – a true taste of Italy in Mexico City.

Fans of Italian food – like myself – had been waiting for a place like Sartoria for ages. While there are many good Italian spots in the city, what chef Marco Carboni – whose résumé includes stints with the likes of Massimo Bottura and Gordon Ramsay – does at this cosy spot is the most beautiful homage to his home country: ingredients are what matter most, especially when they're fresh and handled with love.

A great lunch or dinner at Sartoria might start with some antipasti for the table – a charcuterie platter, marinated olives and the wonderful gnocco frito, a fluffy pastry filled with parmesan foam and topped with prosciutto and balsamic vinegar. Next, of course, a bowl of homemade pasta. If the green tortilla burro e salvia and the spaghetti cacio e pepe are on the menu, do not say no. The extensive wine list covers Italy from the top to the tip of the boot.

The warm hues and the arched ceiling help make Sartoria an extremely welcoming space, though it remains on the smaller side, so reservations are always recommended. And if you're left wanting more, chef Carboni recently opened Bottega Sartoria right across the street – a deli-cum-wine bar where you can buy many of the ingredients he uses here, like charcuterie and pasta, or stop for a glass of wine and a couple of snacks.

Orizaba 42, Roma Norte

Glorieta Insurgentes, line 1
Jardín Pushkin, line 3

Mon–Sat 9am–12.30pm,
1–6.30pm & 7–11pm
Sun 9am–12.30pm
& 1–6.30pm

$MXN

$150–$600

W

sartoria.mx

El Parnita

This always lively and hip restaurant is known for its casual Mexican fare.

Yucatán 84, Roma Norte

Niños Héroes, line 3
Jardín Pushkin, line 3

Tues–Thurs 1–6pm
Fri–Sat 1–7pm, Sun 1–6pm

$MXN

$120–$200

A classic Saturday in Roma Norte includes a stop at this popular eatery, where well-made antojitos (snacks) are served in a kitsch-cool space. The menu here, with many of the recipes passed on by the owners' families, is friendly and uncomplicated.

To start, there are fresh ceviches, and plenty of tacos to choose from. Some of the most popular are El Viajero (pork with avocado) and El Carmelita (fried shrimp, lettuce, red onion) but there are also delicious vegetarian options, like a zucchini flower with Oaxaca cheese combo. Heartier options include tortas and tlacoyos (fried, oval-shaped dishes made of masa and topped with beans, cheese and other ingredients), and part of the fun is spicing everything up with the salsas.

Although the restaurant isn't small, it tends to get quite packed, so make a reservation or get there early. Everybody is welcome here: couples, families and groups of friends of all ages.

Kura

An authentic Japanese izakaya with an excellent menu and plenty of sakes.

Colima 378, Roma Norte

Sevilla, line 1
Durango, line 1

Mon–Sun 11.30am–12am

$MXN

$150–$500

W

kuramexico.com

The Japanese izakaya, a place to come after work for a couple of drinks and a few snacks, translates perfectly here, with plenty of comfortable spaces – from private, tent-like booths upstairs to the bar by the open kitchen. Start by ordering sake from the more than 60 brands available before you explore the extensive menu, courtesy of chef Takeya Matsumoto, who hails from Kanagawa, Japan.

Fresh fish and seafood (like hamachi, salmon, tuna, octopus and ikura) make dishes like sashimi, nigiri and donburi (bowls) excellent options, and there's a particularly interesting dish called the almeja mix, featuring a combination of clam sashimi served on shells. Straight from the grill come all sorts of goodies on sticks, from wagyu to duck to vegetables and the sushi rolls are excellent, too – the spicy soft-shell crab with avocado and eel sauce is especially good. On colder days, go for one of the comforting ramen noodle bowls.

Máximo Bistrot

*The low-key decor hides one of the most memorable
fine-dining experiences in town.*

Sophisticated yet laid-back, with French influences yet decidedly Mexican,
this restaurant made splashes in the city's dining scene when it opened in
2011, bringing its much-needed farm-to-table ethos. Chef Eduardo García's
search for sustainability has guided his vision from the very beginning, and
he can be found personally searching the city's markets and the Xochimilco
chinampas (floating gardens, see p.152) for the freshest ingredients. This
explains why the menu changes every day – in fact, it might change from
lunch to dinner – and why everything tastes exactly as it is supposed to.
In fact, even the furniture – simple yet pretty wooden chairs and tables –
and napkins are sustainably and locally produced.

The meal starts with a hunk of warm bread and fresh butter, and may
include dishes such as pickled beets with caviar and sour cream or caramelised
onions with Comté cheese and black truffle. You can't go wrong with the catch
of the day or the risotto, and desserts never disappoint, either – my passionfruit-
and-meringue combo was a refreshing ending to lunch. The varied wine, mezcal,
and cocktail offerings complete the experience, as does the attentive service
and the lively chatter of the crowd – a mix of locals and visitors who fill the
tables both during the sunny lunches and low-lit dinners. With that in mind,
don't forget to make a reservation a couple of weeks in advance.

Tonala 133, Roma Norte

Hospital General, line 3
Jardín Pushkin, line 3

Tues–Sat
1–5pm & 7–11pm
Sun 1–4pm

$MXN

$120–$500

W

maximobistrot.com.mx

Loup Bar

*Shared food, natural wines, a Parisian
interior ... voila!*

With a passion for natural wines, chef Joaquín Cardoso and French
wine importer Gaëtan Rousset teamed up in 2017 to open this intimate,
comfortable spot. Their goal is to showcase natural wines – those produced
without any intervention – from countries such as Mexico, Italy, France, Chile
and the Czech Republic. The line-up may vary, as Rousset and Cardoso are
always searching for passionate winemakers whose work excites them, but
you're bound to find a variety of red, white and orange wines, as well as
some rosés and bubbly options. And while delving into this world might be
a mystery to some, the staff members are always willing to help, without
overwhelming you with information. At Loup, explains Cardoso, the vibe is not
so much educational as it is convivial.

The food here is meant to be shared, so while you can always choose
your own appetiser and entrée, it's more fun to try a bit of everything. There
are delicious, unfussy options like calamari on toast, tchoutchouka with
organic egg and a wagyu tartare with arugula as appetisers, and hearty
entrées like lamb with couscous and a risotto dish that changes seasonally.
Consider ending your night with a glass of mezcal, as there's also a small but
lovely selection – and it's an excellent digestive.

The restaurant's simple, Parisian-inspired decor – wooden tables,
retro posters and a pretty bar at the end – makes it cosy for small groups and
even better for couples. A candlelit dinner is best followed by a night
of cocktails at Maison Artemisia (see p.117), right upstairs.

Tonalá 23, Roma Norte

Cuauhtémoc, line 1
Álvaro Obregón, line 1

Mon–Wed 4pm–12.30am
Thurs–Sat 1pm–12.30am

$MXN

$90–$270

W

loupbar.mx

El Cardenal

A Mexico City fixture with decades of hospitality and classic Mexican cuisine.

Hilton Mexico City Reforma,
Av. Juárez 70, Centro

Juárez, line 3
Hidalgo, lines 3, 4

Mon–Sun 8am–6.30pm

$MXN

$200–$400

W

restauranteelcardenal.com

A deep love of tradition and hospitality inspired husband-and-wife Jesús Briz and Olivia Garizurieta to open this restaurant back in 1969, in hope of building a family business for their seven kids. To this day, that family warmth remains at all four locations of El Cardenal, but at this particular one, you should note the mural that pays tribute to Diego Rivera's *Sueño de una tarde dominical en la Alameda (Dream of a Sunday afternoon in Alameda)*. The food is comforting and delicious and the team takes special pride in baking their own bread, pastries and tortillas and producing their own cheese and nata (the tasty butterfat they use on desserts and breads).

You must try their foamy hot chocolate, which goes well with their cornbread at dessert or with any pastry at breakfast. It's also the ideal place to try seasonal delicacies, like escamoles (fried and seasoned ant larvae that taste amazing in tacos – in the spring), and chiles en nogada (stuffed poblano chillies with a creamy walnut sauce – in the autumn).

Limosneros

Traditional Mexican fare with clever twists and great insect-based dishes.

Ignacio Allende 3,
Centro Histórico

Allende, line 2
Bellas Artes, line 4

Mon–Sat 1.30–11pm
Sun 1.30–5.30pm

$MXN

$100–$400

W

limosneros.com.mx

When you're born into a famous family, the expectations can be high. Fortunately, Limosneros has lived up to the standards of its parent restaurant, Café de Tacuba, one of the most iconic spots in the city's historic downtown, which has been serving traditional Mexican fare for more than a century. Located just a few steps away, Limosneros is keeping the tradition alive, while updating it with clever twists to classic dishes and a casual-yet-modern atmosphere.

There's an excellent tortilla soup (tomato-based broth with fried tortilla strips, avocado, cheese and chicharrón, or pork rinds), as well as a selection of creative tacos (pork belly, freshwater langoustine, and wagyu beef). But if you're feeling a little adventurous, Limosneros is famous for its insect-based dishes. Try the escamoles (ant larvae) or the cocopaches (beetles sitting on top of goat cheese-stuffed zucchini blossom ravioli) and pair them with a refreshing cocktail to celebrate. La Palmera, with mezcal, pox (a corn-based spirit from Southern Mexico), pineapple, lime and quince candy, is a fine choice.

Azul Histórico

*Renowned chef Ricardo Muñoz Zurita honours
Mexican cuisine in a gorgeous courtyard setting.*

Recognised and beloved for his tireless research on Mexican food, chef Ricardo Muñoz Zurita is the mastermind behind this restaurant, which also has locations in Colonia Condesa and UNAM (National Autonomous University of Mexico). It's safe to say that this is the prettiest one, though, set in the central courtyard of a 17th-century building that also houses the Downtown México hotel and several design stores. The fact that it's right in the heart of the city's historic centre also makes it super popular, which means it's wise to make a reservation a couple of weeks in advance, or walk in a bit before 1pm to secure a table for lunch under the pretty illuminated trees.

On the menu, you'll find excellent dishes that honour Mexican tradition, such as tortilla soup (with chicken and tomato broth, fried tortilla strips, cheese, cream and avocado) and cochinita pibil (pork meat marinated in achiote paste), which tastes even better when served in the warm tortillas that are handmade here – in fact, you can see the tortilla makers expertly making them right next to the bar. Aside from the fixed menu, there are monthly festivals honouring a certain ingredient or region of the country (check the website for details), giving both locals and visitors a reason to come back and try something new time and again.

Isabel la Católica 30,
Centro Histórico

Mon–Sun
9am–12pm & 1–11pm

$MXN
$150–$400

W
azul.rest

Zócalo, line 2; Bellas
Artes, line 8
Isabel la Católica, line 4

Cicatriz

All-day cafe and all-day good vibes with great food and drinks.

Dinamarca 44, Juárez

Cuauhtémoc, line 1
Hamburgo, line 1

Mon–Sun 9am–11pm

$MXN

$120–200

W

cicatrizcafe.com

When they lived in New York City, brother and sister Jake and Scarlett Lindeman worked in the restaurant business, so it was only natural that they'd make use of their talents when they made Mexico City home. That was how Cicatriz was born: a casual, cosy, all-day cafe that quickly became a favourite among locals.

Scarlett's simple, friendly dishes are prepared with excellent ingredients and plenty of house-made goodies, like condiments, sauces and jams. Vegetable-centric options include a lovely plate of roasted carrots with tahini, greens and spicy salsa macha and the kale-based Big Salad, but if you have more of an appetite try the fantastic fried chicken sandwich. As for drinks (Jake's area of expertise), there's a nice selection of natural wines, beer and mezcal, plus great cocktails like the refreshing Yoko, made with mezcal, Aperol, sparkling wine and grapefruit, that are perfect for starting off the evening and watching the place go from cafe to bar, both with a laid-back vibe.

Niddo

Comfort food and a gorgeous setting made this newcomer an instant neighbourhood favourite.

Dresde 2, Juárez

Sevilla, line 1
La Diana, line 7

Tues–Fri 8am–12pm
& 1.30–5pm
Sat 8am–1pm & 2.30–5.30pm
Sun 9am–3pm

$MXN

$150–$250

W

niddo.mx

It's a family affair at this adorable corner cafe, a dream-turned-reality, opened in early 2019 by chef Karen Drijanski, her son Eduardo Plaschinski, and family friend Mauricio Reyes Retana. The soul food–inspired menu features many dishes that pay tribute to Drijanski's Jewish roots, such as the breakfast shakshuka (eggs poached in a sauce of tomato, chilli pepper and spices) and the fluffy babka. Other highlights include the delightful grilled cheese sandwich and the fish cake.

The fresh-baked scones, paired with a cup of coffee from Chiapas, make for perfect company while you wait for a table, which is the most likely scenario. You'll fall instantly in love with the smart interior decoration (by husband-and-wife team Regina Galvanduque and Andrés Mier y Terán), and the Niddo Contigo lifestyle collection, which features edibles like granola and honey, or you can take home a soap, lotion or candles with the house's signature scent.

Amaya

*Simple, smart preparations that let every element
in the dish shine through.*

As one of the most successful chefs in the Baja California region, where his restaurant Laja has been a mainstay for nearly two decades, chef Jair Téllez knows about the importance of working with excellent products and letting them be the stars of the dish. With that philosophy, he opened this casual eatery in Colonia Juárez, one of the city's most rapidly changing areas.

Proof of Téllez's approach are dishes like the incredibly fresh scallop crudo, prepared with cucumbers, cherry tomatos, onions, and sea urchin, and the wagyu picanha (top sirloin), a delicious cut served with sunchoke purée and grilled vegetables.

The food is the perfect excuse for Jair to showcase his very own wines: Bichi — natural wines produced in Tecate, Baja California. His labels are part of a carefully curated list of 'weird wines', as he playfully calls the natural wines from Spain, Italy, Slovenia and Mexico that are available for pairing. But the cocktails that come from behind the long marble bar are worth a try, too. As a tribute to the country's northern region, where the chef was born and raised, they're all named after norteño songs, like the Corazoncito Tirano (which translates as 'Little Tyrant Heart'), a refreshing mix of gin, peppermint, lime juice, coconut water and tonic water. It's all served in an eclectic space, outfitted with pretty mosaic floors and a colourful mural.

General Prim 95, Juárez

Balderas, line 1, 3
París, Route R7

Mon–Sat 1.30–10.30pm
Sun 1–5pm

$MXN

$150–$300

W

amayamexico.com

El Moro

This churro shop opened in the 1930s and has taken over the city (in a great way!).

Génova 59, Juárez

Sevilla, line 1
Glorieta Insurgentes, line 1

Mon–Thurs 7am–11pm
Fri–Sat 7–1am
Sun 8am–11pm

$MXN

$8–$80

W

elmoro.mx

Few things go together as well as churros and hot chocolate, and the Spanish have known this for ages. It was immigrant Francisco Iriarte who blessed us by bringing this tradition with him in the 1930s; first, by wheeling around a churro cart around Zócalo, and later on, by opening a brick-and-mortar shop that quickly drew in a great number of fans, including politicians and writers. His legacy lives on both in the original shop in Centro Histórico, which maintains its old-school charm, and the more than 10 locations that have opened.

While there are indulgent milkshakes and hearty tortas, we're all here for the deep-fried churros, served warm and covered in sugar and cinnamon. There are several styles of hot chocolate, such as Spanish (sweet and thick) and Mexican (a bit lighter), as well as tea and coffee. And if you're feeling particularly indulgent, go for the super-popular Consuelo, an ice-cream sandwich served between two churro twists.

Café Nin

A charming all-day cafe and bakery by Rosetta's chef Elena Reygadas.

Havre 73, Juárez

Cuauhtémoc, line 1
Glorieta Insurgentes, line 1

Mon–Sat 7am–9pm
Sun 7.30am–6pm

$MXN

$90–$300

W

cafenin.com.mx

What started out as an outpost of chef Elena Reygadas' bakeries – Panadería Rosetta – soon expanded into this adorable cafe, as delicious as her other two eateries – Rosetta (see p.57) and Lardo (see p.87), yet with a more casual vibe.

Breakfast options include a black rice pudding with coconut milk and fruit, and fresh juices, including an interesting macadamia-coconut-cardamom blend. But the undeniable stars are the baked goods, like the rosemary-sugar bun or the guava roll.

If you're here for lunch or dinner, the menu includes excellent sandwiches – the roast beef and gruyere is a highlight – and fresh salads, as well as entrées like the soft-shell crab burger. The wine list is a platform for young winemakers from Italy, France and Mexico, and all options are served by the glass. The restaurant's many spaces, especially the bar and the terrace, make it welcoming and lively at any time of day.

Havre 77

A love letter to French brasseries from chef Eduardo García.

The gorgeous building that houses this restaurant is reason enough to make you want to linger. It's so beautiful, in fact, that chef Eduardo García – of Máximo Bistrot (see p.69) and Lalo (see p.60) – and his wife Gabriela López couldn't resist opening a third restaurant when they were offered the space, even though they weren't planning on it. Lucky for us, they did, and the result is this cosy spot where Eduardo pays tribute to the perfect French techniques that so amazed him when he first started cooking.

The short but consistent menu celebrates classic brasserie fare: onion soup, salade Niçoise, moules-frites, a spectacular lobster roll on brioche and creme brûlée, all prepared with excellent ingredients and a flawless technique. But there's much to be enjoyed outside the menu, too as the specials change constantly, depending on what's available in the market. Fresh salads, perfectly cooked fish and hearty soups are always on rotation.

Speaking of fresh, the restaurant boasts an oyster bar, offering lobster, crab, clams and, of course, oysters, which are best paired with a glass of bubbly champagne. Both the oyster bar and the bar in the main dining room are finished with zinc, which, alongside the high ceilings, light pink walls and wooden chairs, gives the space a lovely Parisian feel.

Havre 77, Juárez

Cuauhtémoc, line 1
Hamburgo, line 1

Tues–Sat
1–5pm & 7–11pm
Sun 1–5pm

$MXN

$200–$600

Merkavá

*An Israeli feast so be ready to share and, most of all,
be ready to indulge.*

The flavours of Israel shine at this lively spot in Condesa, the brainchild of chef Daniel Ovadía who, after several successful projects in the city, finally achieved his dream of paying tribute to his roots with this restaurant. At this warm space, decked in light wood and a blue-and-white mural, every meal is meant to be a feast. It's a good idea to go there for lunch or an early dinner, so as not to leave too full, too late.

Start with the Yemeni kubaneh, a fluffy pull-apart bread that comes with tahini butter and a variety of sauces (cumin, tomato, serrano chile) and don't skip the salatim, a parade of tiny salads that can include tabbouleh, falafel, beets and lentils, served with fresh-from-the-oven pita bread. After that, the options are quite varied: hummus is the house specialty (the place is actually called a hummusiya), so there's always an interesting variety, and there are hearty entrées, like the kachapuri, a grilled bread topped with meat, string cheese and egg. End with the babka French toast and a cup of strong coffee.

Make a reservation, as it's usually packed with a cheerful group of fans who include families, couples and locals from the neighbourhood and beyond.

Amsterdam 53, Condesa

Chilpancingo, line 9
Chilpancingo, line 1

Tues–Sat 1pm–12am
Sun 1–6pm

$MXN

$150–$350

Lardo

*Mediterranean-inspired flavours in a beautiful
setting by chef Elena Reygadas.*

After conquering Colonia Roma with her first restaurant, Rosetta (see p.57), chef Elena Reygadas opened her second eatery, the super-cosy Lardo. It's immensely popular from morning to night, so make a reservation or be ready to wait. The casual, welcoming space features an open kitchen with a long bar (perfect for solo diners or couples), as well as comfortable, bare wooden tables set up around it.

At breakfast, start with a steaming cup of tea or a freshly squeezed juice – the pineapple-beet blend is good. Then decide whether you want one of the lighter options, such as baked granola with berries and milk or poached eggs wrapped in hoja santa (a large, aromatic leaf), or something richer, like a croque madame or the crunchy chilaquiles (fried tortilla chips bathed in salsa) with burrata. The lunch and dinner menu showcases the Mediterranean influences in Reygadas' cooking, as seen in the cheese and charcuterie selection, the delightful pizzas and the ever-popular lasagne. For pairing, there's a selection of French, Italian and Mexican wines, all served by the glass, as well as Mexican craft beers. End on a high note with a Lardo classic: the carrot cake and tarragon mille-feuille.

Agustín Melgar 6,
Condesa

Mon–Sat 8am–10.45pm
Sun 8am–5pm

$MXN
$100–$300

W
lardo.mx

Chapultepec, line 1
Chapultepec, line 7

Molino El Pujol

A traditional neighbourhood tortillería by celebrated chef Enrique Olvera.

Benjamín Hill 146, Condesa

Patriotismo, line 9

Patriotismo, line 2

Mon–Sun 8am–5pm

$MXN

$25 for a dozen tortillas

W

pujol.com.mx

An advocate for corn as the soul of Mexican cuisine, chef Enrique Olvera opened this traditional tortillería in 2018. Olvera and his team have joined forces with families from the state of Oaxaca, who supply native corn in many shapes, colours and sizes (used to make masa) and tortillas, sold by the dozen. These efforts seek to promote a healthier and sustainable way to consume corn, as industrial farming has transformed the process over the years.

Stopping by for breakfast or lunch is also an excellent way to take part in this homage to our country's main ingredient. The brief but delicious menu includes tamales and quesadillas in the morning, while at lunchtime, you can treat yourself to corn-on-the-cob with chicatana mayo (a flying ant from Oaxaca), a full-sized version of the baby corn appetiser served at Olvera's famed restaurant Pujol (see p.93). Pair with a cold La Bru, a craft beer that hails from Michoacán and is made with – what else? – corn.

Pasillo de Humo

Authentic Oaxacan flavours (and plenty of mezcal) in a laid-back atmosphere.

Mercado Parián Condesa,
Nuevo León 107, Condesa

Chilpancingo, line 9
Campeche, line 1

Mon–Wed 9am–10pm
Thurs–Sat 9am–11pm
Sun 9am–7pm

$MXN

$100–$350

The fascinating, complex flavours of the state of Oaxaca await at this casual eatery, where young chef Alam Méndez showcases many of the state's greatest specialties.

Among the many delicious options, don't skip the tlayudas (an extra-large tortilla topped with beans, avocado, chorizo, Oaxaca cheese and grasshoppers) or the molotes itsmeños (plantain croquettes stuffed with cheese and bathed in mole – a complex sauce that can include dozens of ingredients). And speaking of mole, Méndez offers several excellent versions of this most sacred of Mexican dishes, including black, yellow and almendrado (almond-based). The most natural pairing option is mezcal, another gift from Oaxaca to the world. The bottles are brought to your table in a cute cart.

If you're here for breakfast, ask for a hot cup of chocolate de agua and a fluffy pan de yema (an airy bread made with egg yolks). If you're feeling particularly indulgent, take a look around the food hall on the ground level and get an extra treat.

Quintonil

*Contemporary Mexican fine dining with a focus
on fresh, seasonal ingredients.*

Named after an herb that is particularly appreciated in central Mexico, chef
Jorge Vallejo's restaurant is quite beloved, thanks to its clever approach
to Mexican flavours and techniques. By putting a special focus on fresh,
seasonal ingredients (especially vegetables that come from the restaurant's
own garden or the Xochimilco chinampas, see p.152), Vallejo's ever-changing
menu never ceases to impress. And while there are constant surprises both
on the à la carte and the tasting menu, there are a few mainstays that
perfectly represent the Quintonil philosophy, like the charred avocado tartare
with escamoles (ant larvae), the crab tostada with radish and habanero mayo,
and the mamey panna cotta.

Aside from a long wine list that includes options from Mexico, the
United States, France, Spain and Argentina, there is a top selection of spirits,
plus interesting cocktails that are named after classic Mexican songs, like the
bourbon-and-watermelon Cielo Rojo.

It's smart to make a reservation a few weeks in advance, as the dining
room – intimate and simply decorated – tends to always be busy with people
on business lunches, dates and group dinners. Once you're here, you can be
sure service will be excellent, as Alejandra Flores, Vallejo's wife, is in charge
of the front of the house.

Isaac Newton 55, Polanco

Polanco, line 7

Mon–Sat

1–4pm & 6.30–10pm

$MXN

$150–$600

(tasting menu $2250;

with pairing $3650)

W

quintonil.com

Pujol

*Celebrated chef Enrique Olvera's groundbreaking restaurant
proves that it's possible to improve on perfection.*

What can you say about Pujol that hasn't been said before? Plenty. Chef Enrique Olvera founded this restaurant back in 2000, and he has built quite the reputation since then, but that doesn't mean that he has rested on his laurels. These days, his landmark restaurant remains as fascinating and delicious as ever.

Eating here means trusting the kitchen entirely – it's a tasting menu only and there are two versions: one inspired by the sea (with dishes like striped bass with hoja santa and tomato jam) and the other inspired by corn (featuring creations like sweet potato with pine nut mole sauce). A third option is the very fun taco omakase: a 10-course parade of handheld treats, like a lobster taco on an hoja santa tortilla and served with interesting pairings, including sake, mezcal and wine. All three menus feature Olvera's legendary mole sauces (a complex sauce featuring many ingredients): mole madre and mole nuevo, a 36–ingredient mole that has been ageing for around 1900 days (and counting!), topped with a dollop of freshly cooked mole. Whichever you choose, make sure you make a reservation at least two or three months in advance.

The gorgeous surroundings – take notice of the terrace, with lush greenery and pretty fire pits – come courtesy of architect Javier Sánchez, while the playlists are curated by Olvera himself.

Tennyson 133, Polanco

Polanco, line 7
Campo Marte, line 7

Mon–Sat 1.30–10.45pm

$MXN

$2227 for corn tasting menu, $2554 for sea tasting menu, $3332 for taco tasting menu

W

pujol.com.mx

Salón Ríos

The traditional cantina gets a modern twist at this always fun restaurant–bar.

Río Lerma 218, Cuauhtémoc

Sevilla, line 1
La Palma, line 7

Mon–Sat 12pm–3am
Sun 12pm–8pm

$MXN

$45–$300

W

salonrios.mx

There's never a bad time to go to this lively venue. Since it opened in 2016, this modern take on the cantina – a bar where guests can order antojitos (snacks) to pair with their drink of choice – has offered good food and drinks at good prices. But no cantina has ever looked as cool as Salón Ríos, with its tropical wallpaper, wooden ceiling and the crown jewel: an impressive, multi-shelved bar right in the middle of the room.

As soon as you sit down, you'll be welcomed with a cup of spicy shrimp broth and a taco de canasta (a small, soft taco stuffed with duck), after which comes the real fun: ordering drinks and appetisers, followed by another round. Highlights include the cochinita pibil torta and excellent soft-shell crab tacos. As for drinks, there's refreshing margarita made with mezcal and a solid spirit selection. Afterwards, head upstairs to their dance club, El Babalú, and salsa the night away.

Rokai

Authentic Japanese cuisine where fresh fish and seafood dictate the menu.

Río Ebro 87, Cuauhtémoc

Sevilla, line 1
La Palma, line 7

Mon–Sat 1–11pm
Sun 12pm–6pm

$MXN

$150–$1200

W

edokobayashi.com

Few dining experiences are as exciting as an omakase: trusting a chef with serving you whatever they choose. That's one of the main reasons to visit this Japanese spot, where the freshest fish and seafood (mostly from Mexican waters) dictate the night's courses, including sushi, sashimi and soup. But on the regular menu, you'll find a nigiri platter that's almost too beautiful to eat, with delicacies like toro, kampachi and chocolate clam; crunchy shrimp tempura; and pork gyozas.

Sake, beer, wine and cocktails are yours for pairing and while many dishes are perfect for sharing, this is not the most group-friendly space, as it gets crowded. In fact, it's always smart to make a reservation. The restaurant's simple yet balanced and detailed decor makes it quite cosy and confirms the clear understanding that its owners, the Edo Kobayashi group, have of Japanese food and its culture, earning them a band of loyal followers.

Los Danzantes

At this neighbourhood mainstay, mezcal and Mexican flavours guarantee a great afternoon.

Plaza Jardín Centenario 12, Coyoacán

Mon–Wed
12.30pm–11pm
Thurs 12.30pm–12am
Fri–Sat 9–2am
Sun 9am–11pm

$MXN

$120–$300

W

losdanzantes.com

A Coyoacán institution, this restaurant has been welcoming guests since 1995. It's a great spot for exploring the world of mezcal, as it belongs to Grupo Los Danzantes, one of the most respected mezcal producers in the country. You can also go for a cocktail, like the fruity Hecho un Mango.

The menu is packed with earthy, traditional flavours, best expressed in the house classics, like the Hoja Santa, a large aromatic leaf stuffed with Oaxaca and goat cheeses and served on a chilli-and-miltomate (green tomato) sauce, or the ravioli stuffed with huitlacoche (corn mushrooms) and bathed in a creamy poblano chile sauce. Salads are prepared with vegetables grown in the restaurant's own chinampas (floating gardens) in Xochimilco (see p.152), so freshness is guaranteed.

The laid-back, welcoming atmosphere makes it an excellent spot for groups, but always make a reservation.

Terraza Cha Cha Chá

Great drinks and shareable snacks with an amazing view and atmosphere.

De la República 157, Tabacalera

Revolución, line 2
Plaza de la República, line 4

Mon–Sat
1.30pm–12am
Sun 1.30–7pm

$MXN

$100–$350

W

grupopalmares.com.mx

For most locals, Acapulco has been a favourite tropical getaway for decades. And it's the bay's golden age that inspired the vibe for this laid-back terrace, which offers an incomparable view of Monumento a la Revolución (see p.155). Opened in 2018, the restaurant has quickly become a favourite hangout, so it's always a good idea to make a reservation.

The extensive, unpretentious menu features an array of Mexican antojitos (snacks) that are ideal for sharing, like duck tacos, fresh tuna tostadas, ceviches and aguachiles, as well as entrées like pulpo arrebatado (marinated octopus) or a pork shank that's great for DIY tacos. There's lively music and atmosphere and plenty of spirits to choose from – mezcal, tequila, rum, whiskey – and a fun cocktail menu (highlights include the mezcal-based margarita with xoconostle, the fruit that grows on cacti). If you spot the bartender rolling the gin and tonic cart, stop him for a refreshing treat.

Nicos

At this welcoming venue, Mexican cuisine is served with a deep love for tradition.

Av. Cuitláhuac 3102, Clavería

Cuitláhuac, line 2

Mon–Fri
7.30am–12:30pm & 1pm–7pm
Sat 8am–12pm & 1.30pm–7pm

$MXN

$125–$350

W

nicosmexico.mx

Mother-and-son team María Elena Lugo Zermeño and Gerardo Vázquez Lugo run this restaurant with a shared passion for traditional Mexican food. When Vázquez Lugo took over in 2006, he started a fascinating new era for the restaurant, maintaining a deep respect for traditional recipes and bringing in the principles of the Slow Food movement.

One of the most enjoyable parts of your meal will be all the tableside action: during breakfast, ask for café con leche and watch how they pour the milk from way up high. At lunch, the caesar salad and the guacamole will also become a little spectacle for you to enjoy. Other good breakfast decisions are the huevo encamisado ('eggs in a shirt', as the egg is cooked inside a tortilla), while at lunch the goat cheese soup, made with artisanal goat cheese from Querétaro, is one of many winners. The unfussy, familiar atmosphere and excellent mezcal selection will make you feel right at home.

Carmela y Sal

The flavours of Tabasco get a creative and sophisticated touch.

Torre Virreyes, Pedregal 24,
Lomas Virreyes

Mon–Wed 1–11pm
Thurs–Sat 1–11.30pm
Sun 1–7pm

$MXN
$120–$420

W
carmelaysal.mx

Young chef Gabriela Ruiz brings the flavours of her native state of Tabasco to this elegant space, with high ceilings, dark wood and touches of velvet. While the restaurant is in an office building in a mostly residential neighbourhood, it's only a short drive from Bosque de Chapultepec park, and definitely worth a detour.

The poetic menu is divided as if it were a concert: in the Prelude section, try the 'fake tostadas', topped with prepared coconut instead of protein (the coconut is ripened until it reaches the necessary texture), and don't skip the octopus-and-chicharrón sope when you get to the Interlude. The entrées are under Climax, where you'll find mouth-watering short rib with chilmole (a slight spicy, smoked sauce), and the Outro has treats like bananas with cream, dulce de leche and caramel dust. The interesting cocktail menu, developed by bartender Jan Van Ongevalle from Belgium's The Pharmacy, includes The Estragón, with mezcal, grilled pineapple and absinthe, a potent and refreshing concoction.

Loretta Chic Bistrot

*Field-inspired flavours and an excellent wine
selection make this restaurant a worthy destination.*

A tribute to the gifts of nature in the middle of the city, this restaurant is
the result of a joint effort between chef Abel Hernández, known for his clever
twists on French cuisine, and renowned sommelier Laura Santander. Opening
the extensive menu packed with Mediterranean-inspired creations hints at
a few hard decisions to come, but luckily, most dishes are perfect for sharing.
Appetisers like a grilled oyster with butter and parmesan cheese, sobrasada-
stuffed dates wrapped in pancetta and a light tuna crudo show that bright,
powerful flavours and an excellent cooking technique are the theme here.

Entrées like mushrooms in parmesan fonduta and lamb moussaka
confirm this theory, especially when paired with wines from the list carefully
curated by Santander, featuring Old World finds from Bulgaria or Croatia.
And make sure you save room for dessert – the light and creamy cheesecake
baklava is a beauty.

The sleek decor and the attentive service make it easy to lose track
of time, especially if you're sitting in the charming terrace. And while it can
be a bit of a hike to get here (the neighbourhood isn't exactly a tourist
hotspot), it's definitely worth a detour, perhaps on your way back from
Xochimilco chinampas (floating gardens, see p.152) or San Ángel.

Av. Revolución 1426,
Guadalupe Inn

Mon–Sat 2–11pm
Sun 2–6pm

$MXN

$180–$300

Sud 777

The beautiful space, with several rooms and a terrace, is as sophisticated as the technique displayed in every dish.

Since he was a little kid, chef Edgar Nuñez was one of those kids who loved vegetables, and he has his mother to thank for that. His passion for natural ingredients shows in his creations at his fine-dining restaurant, located in a residential neighbourhood in the southern part of the city.

To execute his contemporary Mexican cuisine, Nuñez makes sure that every ingredient used was grown or raised in the country. The vegetables, for example, come from the Xochimilco chinampas (floating gardens, see p.152) or from the restaurant's own garden. This focus on freshness also means that the menu changes constantly: the á la carte offerings change four times a month, while the tasting menu changes every month or so.

Creations may include a homemade burrata in salsa verde or a perfectly cooked duck with mole (sauce) amarillo, endives and a sweet potato purée. And the food is not just delicious – it's visually stunning, too. The wine list focuses on bottles from countries like Mexico, Italy, France, Spain and the United States, but you can also ask for a non-alcoholic pairing and try the interesting juices instead.

Reservations are strongly recommended, so call a couple of weeks in advance.

Blvd. de la Luz 777,
Jardines del Pedregal

Mon–Sat 2pm–12am
Sun 1.30–6pm

$MXN

$180–$500 (per dish);
$1500 tasting menu

W

sud777.com.mx

Fonda Margarita

*A hearty, traditional Mexican breakfast that
is worth getting up at dawn for.*

Hailed by many as the greatest breakfast in the city, this modest eatery promises no glamourous lingering brunches; no Instagram-worthy bowls or pretty lattes. Just amazing food. Open at the crack of dawn, the restaurant draws the most varied of crowds: from families and friends to groups of younger people who are wrapping up after a long night of partying. They all share the long communal tables, adorned with nothing but metal napkin holders and baskets of warm tortillas.

The menu is hanging on the wall but you can always go check out what the ladies with the steaming cazuelas are up to if you're trying to decide what to order. Foolproof options include chicharrón en verde (pork rinds in a green sauce), steak in pasilla chile sauce, frijoles refritos con huevo (eggs scrambled with black beans) and excellent chilaquiles in green or red salsa. Go for the grand finale with an order of churros and a cup of hot café de olla, coffee prepared with cinnamon and whole cane sugar.

This hearty breakfast, surrounded by the chatter of fellow early birds and the live band playing at the end of the room, can be a good omen for the rest of your day.

Adolfo Prieto 1364B,
Del Valle

Tues–Sun 5.30–11.30am

$MXN

$40–$80

Hospital 20 de
Noviembre, line 12
Parque Hundido, line 1

A QUICK GUIDE
TO STREET FOOD

Everyone in Mexico City has their favourite street-food spots and they will swear by them, you will hear people saying things like: this is the place for tacos after a night out; this lady makes the greatest tortas in the neighbourhood; your life won't be the same after trying these carnitas.

Street food is something we take very seriously and keep close to our hearts, and that makes it all the more satisfying. Sometimes hunger isn't even an issue – the smell of a good treat on the footpath (sidewalk) will be enough to make you change your eating schedule for the day.

During your visit, you'll spot stands, carts and more established restaurants selling everything you could ever imagine: from giant juices and sliced fruit, to hot dogs and every possible kind of taco. The rule of thumb is just to make sure that places look clean, but most of all, that whatever you're about to eat looks mouth-watering to you and that you spot a nice amount of locals eating there, too. Here I have listed my recommended street-food sellers but you'll find these foods pretty much all over the city.

Tacos al Pastor

Brought to Mexico by Lebanese immigrants, these are distant cousins of the shawarma but we have completely adopted them as our own. The pork meat is seasoned with dried chillies and spices and cooked to perfection on a vertical spit, then served on small corn tortillas. Classic toppings include cilantro (coriander), onions and sliced pineapple.

El Tizoncito (Tamaulipas 122, Condesa)

Cochinita Pibil

This crown jewel from the Yucatán region is a favourite filling for tacos, tortas, and other masa-based treats. The pork meat is prepared with a mix called achiote – it includes achiote seeds, plus spices like oregano, black pepper, clove, cumin and bitter orange – and cooked inside banana leaves until very soft. A couple of slices of red onion helps cut through the fat.

El Turix (Emilio Castelar 212, Polanco)

Tortas

The whole world can fit between two pieces of bread and a good torta will always feature some kind of protein – be it ham, pork, milanesa, cheese or a combination of these. Then add a fair amount of accompaniments, which can include avocado slices, mayonnaise, tomato slices, beans and some type of chilli, like chipotle or poblano.

La Delicia (Prado Norte 403, Lomas de Chapultepec)

Carnitas

The secret behind these super-tasty, small cuts of pork is that they're braised in lard. A healthy mix of carnitas usually includes several cuts, like costillitas (ribs), maciza (boneless meat from the leg or loin) and cueritos (fried skin). They are best enjoyed in tacos with your preferred salsa and a few drops of lime.

El Rincón Tarasco (José Martí 142, Escandón)

Interesting Tacos

As mentioned before, you can find all kinds of delicious and creative tacos across the city, and these ones are a clever wink to traditional Peking duck wraps. The soft, baked duck is served in handmade flour tortillas and you can choose from a more traditional version, with plum sauce, or a carnitas-inspired one, with beans and epazote.

El Auténtico Pato Manila (Culiacán 91, Condesa)

BARS

The locals love to gather around the table with a drink in hand. It's a perfect excuse to spend quality time with friends or family, and this warmth is on display whenever you visit a bar in the city.

The wide array of watering holes on offer – you can go to a sophisticated speakeasy or a super-casual mezcal dive – is a reflection of the city's diverse and eclectic personality, and of the impressive speed at which the bar scene has developed over the past few years. Interestingly, although Mexico is home to centuries-old spirits, such as tequila, mezcal and raicilla – and a visit to the city is the perfect excuse to try them all – our bar culture has had a bit of a hard time keeping up. Luckily, a wave of visionary bartenders and entrepreneurs have taken charge, adding a variety of bars that not only compete with their international counterparts but, most importantly, are incredibly fun. Whether it's for a night of tropical concoctions at Waikiki Tiki Room (see p.115), or an evening of pre-Hispanic-inspired creations at Xaman (see p.122), you'll always have an excuse to stay out a bit longer.

Licorería Limantour

The city's pioneer of top-quality cocktails.

A decade ago, when rum-and-cokes and fruity martinis were the norm in most bars in town, Limantour came in to shake things up (pun intended!). Setting up shop in a gorgeous two-level house in Roma Norte, its team of superstar bartenders taught locals how to wait patiently for a properly shaken cocktail, prepared with ingredients like high-quality spirits, fresh juices and homemade bitters.

Over the years, the bar's reputation has grown steadily, earning it high spots on prestigious international lists, as its team members – like José Luis León – constantly make stellar appearances in bartending competitions. Yet none of this means that fame has erased the bar's easygoing essence – it remains a solid favourite among a diverse crowd of locals and visitors of all ages. The atmosphere helps, too. The bar is quite lively all week long, but the music and chatter always allow for conversation to flow; while the two-level space, with Art Deco touches, means there's plenty of room to mingle, though it's not a bad idea to make a reservation.

I keep coming back for the ever-inspired cocktail selection, featuring house favourites like the Mr Pink (gin, grapefruit, lime, rosemary syrup and basil) or inventive creations that change seasonally. The staff's constant travels, plus their frequent collaborations with colleagues – Limantour loves hosting visiting bartenders from Mexico and all over the world – keep them inspired, and that shows on each page of the menu.

There is also a second location in Polanco (Oscar Wilde 9).

Alvaro Obregón 106,
Roma Norte

Niños Héroes, line 3
Jardín Pushkin, line 3

Mon & Tues 6pm–12am
Wed 6pm–1am
Thurs–Sat 6pm–2am
Sun 6–11pm

$MXN
$120–$200 per cocktail

Can Can

Board games and entertainment pair with casual food and drinks.

Durango 175, Roma Norte

Sevilla, line 1
Jardín Pushkin, line 3

Tues–Sat 1pm–2am

$MXN

$80–$160 per cocktail

The easiest way to describe this laid-back bar would be to think of your best friend's living room – if it were huge and had the most incredibly stocked bar, of course. This super-casual space is perfect for small and large groups who want to play board games, watch a soccer match or a live music performance, or challenge each other to a foosball tournament.

When it comes to the menu, the offerings are equally casual – yet extremely fun. Try the French fries, prepared with aioli, fetta cheese, fennel and house-made vinegar, or the grilled cheese sandwich with longaniza (spicy pork sausage) and a touch of cayenne pepper. Pair your food with an unpretentious cocktail, like a Long Island iced tea or a refreshing Salmoncito (gin, Campari, grapefruit, tonic water). You'll also find a selection of craft beer and natural wines.

Bar Oriente

Dance and sing the night away at this fun club.

Durango 181, Roma Norte

Sevilla, Line 1
Jardín Pushkin, line 3

Wed—Sat 9pm—3am

$MXN
$120–$200 per cocktail

W
oriente.bar

Good drinks, singing and dancing – all under one roof. This multi-level club packs a full night of fun in an unpretentious yet hip atmosphere. The decor – neon signs in the karaoke rooms, an all-white smoking area/ sake-tasting room – is as cool as the crowd it attracts: young people who seem to never run out of energy.

On the dance floor, you can dance to salsa and reggae or watch a drag show. Performances are always eclectic and fun. And if you're more interested in performing yourself, book one of the two karaoke rooms, and let your talents shine – make sure you book a couple of weeks in advance through the Open Table website.

Waikiki Tiki Room

Drinks at this tropical joint feel like a beach getaway.

For all of its varied drinking options, this city was in desperate need of a tiki-inspired oasis. Is there a better way to mentally escape from your big-city reality than having a tropical cocktail and listening to reggae? Luckily, the creative duo of designer Walter Meyenberg (who has also worked on hotspots like Hanky Panky, see p.121) and chef Tomás Bermúdez (of La Docena fame see p.56) heard the call from the tropics, and opened this laid-back, colourful spot in early 2019. With its Hawaiian-themed murals, neon signs and wicker lamps, you'll immediately be transported to an island where time seems to go by at a much slower pace. The carefully curated playlist features only the most chilled tunes – a little reggae, a little Bee Gees.

 The drinks menu features classic tiki libations like the Zombie, a powerful blend of four rums – from Oaxaca, Barbados, Jamaica and Trinidad and Tobago; green Chartreuse (absinthe, grapefruit, lime juice, orgeat) and Angostura. The crowning moment comes when the bartender places a shot of rum on top and sets it on fire, making it a spectacle to watch – and drink. Less flashy – but equally delicious – options include the Stumblebee, made with tequila, lime juice and honey. The food menu by Bermúdez, features snacks like ceviches and crab wontons, a fine pairing to complete this island getaway. If you want a quick drink in the evening, you'll find that the place is quite calm, but it gets busier around 8pm, so call beforehand to secure your table.

Orizaba 115, Roma Norte

Tues–Sat 5pm–2am

$MXN

$120–$250 per cocktail

Niños Héroes, line 3
Alvaro Obregón, line 1

Casa Franca

Live music and strong drinks await at this relaxed bar.

📍

Mérida 109, Roma Norte

/

Cuauhtémoc, line 1
Jardín Pushkin, line 3

🕐

Tues–Wed 5pm–1am
Thurs–Sat 5pm–2am

$MXN

$150–$200 per drink

From street level, Casa Franca might seem like a cosy restaurant in which to enjoy a slice of pizza and a glass of wine. And it is. But if you look closely, there's a stairway that will lead you upstairs to a multi-room space which is filled with the sounds of live music every night.

Outfitted with rich wallpapers, vintage furniture, elegant lamps and flower vases, the atmosphere is relaxed and welcoming, as people gather here to enjoy live performances that include jazz, blues, funk and soul, featuring bands and solo artists from Mexico and abroad. At the bar, you can choose from a selection of spirits like whiskey and mezcal, craft beers, and strong, classic cocktails or house creations, cleverly named after jazz legends. It's perfect for a date or a night out with a small group of friends.

Maison Artemisia

Absinthe and specialty cocktails flow at this romantic bar.

Tonalá 23, Roma Norte

Cuauhtémoc, line 1
Jardín Pushkin, line 3

Tues–Sat 7.30pm–2am

$MXN

$120-$250 per cocktail

W

maisonartemisia.com

People don't just stumble into this intimate watering hole. Those who walk to the second floor of this early 20th-century house know that great things happen behind the bar. Artemisia is the only bar in Mexico City that specialises in absinthe – in fact, they pour their own Absinthe Artemisia, made in Pontalier, France, while also placing a strong focus on Mexican sprits such as mezcal, sotol and raicilla.

The low lighting and romantic decor – velvet chairs, crystal chandeliers – combined with the eclectic music line-up, which can include everything from live jazz to burlesque, make it an excellent spot for a date night, especially if you have dinner at Loup Bar (located right downstairs, see p.71) before your head here for a few cocktails.

Bósforo

*The ultimate destination to explore
the world of mezcal.*

Mezcal is surrounded by a certain air of mystery and a couple of urban legends – some say it's an aphrodisiac, others say it has an effect similar to LSD. To judge for yourself, step into this dark bar, where mezcal is the drink that rules them all. The bartenders will be happy to walk beside you in your journey, just be ready to sacrifice your personal space for the sake of knowledge and enjoyment. (No joke, sometimes you might end up sitting on the floor.)

Under the cover of dim lighting and an eclectic world-music playlist, ask about the more than 40 kinds of artisanal mezcal available: the type of agave – do you want to try the smoother espadín or an aromatic tobalá?; the region where it came from – should you explore Oaxaca or perhaps Durango?; or the level of smokiness. A couple of drinks later, you'll understand why this spot is a favourite among local intellectuals and hospitality industry insiders.

There's a solid selection of Mexican food, too. Especially popular are the blue-corn quesadillas, in versions like plain cheese or stuffed with chapulines (fried grasshoppers).

Luis Moya 31,
Centro Histórico

Tues–Sat 6pm–2am

$MXN
$100–$200 per drink

Juárez, line 3;
Bellas Artes, lines 2, 8
Juárez, line 3

Bars

Hanky Panky

A hidden, sexy space serving high-end cocktails.

Ever since it opened its doors in 2017, there was a buzz around this speakeasy. Where was it? How hard was it to score a seat at the bar? Even now the address remains a secret, with only a phone number to ring to find out its location. And while smart cocktail lovers have learned the tricks over the years, there's still something special about crossing the secret door, hidden in the back of a little venue in the neighbourhood of Colonia Juárez, and discovering this sleek, sexy space, where it feels like nobody can find you.

The red leather booths are perfect for small groups, while positioning yourself at the long marble bar will give you a front-row seat to the shaking-and-stirring action. Choose your poison from one of the two cocktail menus: timeless classics, like the drink that gives the bar its name (a strong, aromatic mix of gin, vermouth rosso and Fernet Branca) and signature drinks, created by a team of star bartenders, like Ricardo Sandoval (Mexico) and Natalie Migliarini (USA), that might feature all sorts of interesting ingredients, from traditional Mexican candy to saffron or hibiscus.

If you get hungry, there's a full bar-food menu, courtesy of chef Maycoll Calderón (of Colonia Roma's Huset), featuring treats like sashimi and short ribs.

Secret Location

Tues–Sat 6.30pm–2am

$MXN
$150–$250 per cocktail

Cuauhtémoc, line 1
Reforma, line 7

55 9155 0958
for reservations and
directions

W
hankypanky.mx

Xaman

Potent cocktails inspired by Mexican botanicals.

Copenhague 6, Juárez

Cuauhtémoc, line 1
La Palma, line 7

Tues–Wed 6pm–12am
Thurs–Sat 6pm–2am

$MXN

$120–$200 per cocktail

The art of Mexican botanicals inspires the liquid concoctions at this speakeasy, many of which are based on local spirits like tequila and mezcal. Mixed with the ingredients from the dozens of jars behind the bar, the results are always interesting – it's not for nothing that the name of the bar is pronounced 'shaman'.

Cocktails can go from sweet, like the tequila-based Tea Time (tequila, pineapple tea, lemon bitters, agave syrup, lime and Poblano chile liquor) to super spicy, like El Crudandero (mezcal, Cointreau, Aperol, lime juice, cilantro, agave syrup, chilli, tonic water), which is said to cure even the worst of hangovers. The drinks stay strong as the vibe progresses from chilled in the evening to clubbier later at night.

Baltra

*Perfectly poured drinks
in an intimate atmosphere.*

Iztaccíhuatl 36D, Condesa

Chilpancingo, line 9
Campeche, line 1

Mon–Tues 6pm–12am
Wed 6pm–1am
Thurs–Sat 6pm–2am
Sun 6–11pm

$MXN

$120–250 per cocktail

W
baltra.bar

Named after one of the Galapagos islands that Charles Darwin visited during his expeditions, this cosy little hideout takes the concept of evolution as its inspiration, pouring inventive drinks in a most inviting atmosphere. The intimate lighting, the soft music and the thoughtful decor – with illustrations and framed insects – set the mood for discovery.

Heading to the bar to ask for ideas is your best bet. The bartender might suggest one of the many kinds of mezcal in stock (categorised by type of agave, alcohol content or region) or a classic cocktail – the Negroni and the vodka martini are excellent here, and something from the always interesting seasonal menu, which changes every six months. A recent menu was inspired by an Oxford University textbook from Darwin's times, and featured an intriguing milk punch made with rum and marsala wine.

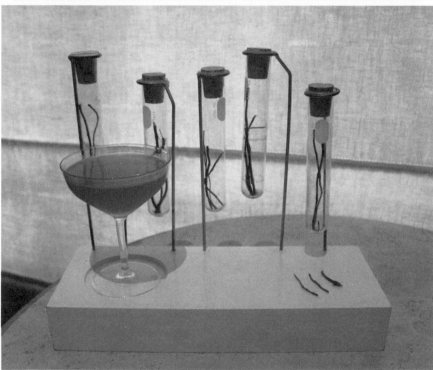

Fifty Mils

Creative cocktails inside the Four Seasons Hotel.

As one of the busiest and most beloved hotels in town, the Four Seasons needed an excellent bar to complete its dining offerings and Fifty Mils has lived up to the expectation since it opened its doors at the end of 2015. Not only is the decor as sophisticated as one would expect from this luxury hotel – a long marble bar and rich velvet touches that echo the feeling of a British country house – but the cocktails featured are the result of constant experimentation, as delicious as they are fun to try.

Clever creations like the Frijolito (tequila, bean-and-bourbon puree, lime, chile liquor, agave syrup, tonic water) and the Inside Manhattan (bourbon, Martini rosso, Martini bianco, Cynar, Angostura bitters) have earned its talented team recognition in local and international competitions and have quickly turned the hotel into a favourite hangout among locals, as well as visitors. It doesn't hurt that it also boasts a lovely courtyard and a private little garden with a fire pit – you'll love it for your social media posts. The crowd is always diverse and on a regular night you'll find a mix of business travellers, couples and young locals, all gathered by their appreciation of a well-served cocktail.

Four Seasons Mexico
City, Reforma 500,
Cuauhtémoc

Mon–Sat 12pm–2am
Sunday 12pm–12am

$MXN
$150–$250 per cocktail

W
fiftymils.com

Sevilla, Chapultepec,
line 1
Chapultepec, line 7

Tokyo Music Bar

A sleek space to enjoy good music and good drinks.

A recent addition to the Mexico City landscape, this space is dedicated to one of the greatest pleasures in life: listening to good music while having a great drink. Sounds simple, but it's not. The masterminds behind the concept are the Edo Kobayashi group (also responsible for spots like Le Tachinomi Desu downstairs, see p.128 and Rokai, a few steps away, see p.95). For starters, the music doesn't just come out from any old set of speakers. This is a 'hi-fi analog audio cocktail bar', meaning that every note you hear comes courtesy of a 1970s McIntosh system and a set of Tannoy Westminster speakers. Every evening, the bartenders start choosing records from the varied collection until 9pm, when a music selector (DJ) comes in and takes over the booth. Tunes can go from new wave to jazz to Japanese pop, depending on the crowd and its mood.

There's been as much thought put into the drinks, which are served in exquisite Japanese glasses. Classic cocktails, like the potent dry martini, are prepared with textbook recipes, while house libations show creativity and perfect techniques. The Champagne Coast, for example, is a sweet blend of champagne, bee pollen and calvados.

Call a few days in advance to book your table, and keep in mind that the bar only welcomes groups of six or fewer. Grab a seat at the beautiful wooden bar or at one of the green marble tables, and take in every detail: the pink velvet chairs, the custom-made chocolates, the chilled, sophisticated vibe.

Río Pánuco 132,
first floor, Cuauhtémoc

Sevilla, Chapultepec,
line 1
Chapultepec, line 7

Mon–Sat 6pm–2am

$MXN
$250 per drink

W
edokobayashi.com

Le Tachinomi Desu

A sake and wine joint inspired by Japanese standing bars.

Río Pánuco 132, Cuauhtémoc

Sevilla, Chapultepec, line 1
Chapultepec, line 7

Mon–Sat 7pm–2am

$MXN

$120–$500 per drink

W

edokobayashi.com

You'll be too busy enjoying yourself at this wine and sake bar to miss the seats. In Japanese, tachi means stand and nomi means drink, and this tiny spot is modelled after Japan's standing bars.

Sake, Japanese wine and whiskey, as well as Mexican and Japanese craft beer, make up the liquid offerings, while the food menu changes daily. Choose from a selection of dishes or trust the chef and go for the three-course omakase (meaning, I'll leave it up to you). Expect surprises like a tuna crudo or an aged duck-and-foie tostada (crispy wonton). The bar has room only for 18 guests so although walk-ins are welcome, it's wise to make a reservation.

If you're in the area between 8am and 3pm, the space is transformed into Enomoto Café, serving classic Japanese sandos (the fried pork Tonkatsu is not to be missed) and coffee.

King Cole Bar

Great views and posh drinks inside the St. Regis Hotel.

The St Regis Mexico City,
Paseo de la Reforma 439,
Cuauhtémoc

Sevilla, line 1
La Diana, line 7

Mon–Sat 11–2am
Sun 11–1am

$MXN

$200–$300 per cocktail

W

stregis.com

The Bloody Mary was born at the original King Cole Bar in New York City's St. Regis in the 1930s. Since then, the hotel brand has established a wonderful tradition, developing an original Bloody Mary recipe at each of its locations. Here in Mexico City, the Sangrita María is spiked with mezcal and pasilla chile paste. But this is just one of many reasons that you should visit the sophisticated bar. Located on the third floor of the St Regis and offering fantastic views of Paseo de la Reforma, the bar is divided into two areas. Inside, velvet sofas and a piano create the perfect atmosphere for enjoying a single-malt whiskey; out on the terrace, the wicker chairs call for a refreshing cocktail.

The creative team of bartenders is always ready to shake up something to suit your tastebuds, whether it's one of their creations or a foolproof version of a classic – the best Moscow Mule in town, probably. If you're feeling particularly energetic, come in on a Friday or Saturday night, when a live DJ is playing.

HISTORIC + CULTURAL ATTRACTIONS

Mexico City is home to more than 150 cultural institutions, some of which you'll find in this chapter and others in the Modern + Contemporary Art chapter (see p. 159). Many of these are concentrated in certain neighbourhoods, like Centro Histórico and Bosque de Chapultepec, making navigation easy. In a day, you can explore Museo del Templo Mayor (see p. 135), a major Aztec site and then delve into human rights at Museo Memoria y Tolerancia (see p. 141). You can discover pre-Hispanic cultures, like the Maya, at Museo Nacional de Antropología (see p. 147) or the fascinating former home of Frida Kahlo, at Museo Frida Kahlo (see p. 149).

Maintaining Mexico City's reputation as one of the museum capitals of the world takes work, and these museums take pride in providing guided tours and offering affordable entrance fees. In fact, many of them are free, or free on certain days.

Museo Nacional de Arte (MUNAL)

A palatial setting for the treasures stored inside.

Even before you learn what's inside this gorgeous palace, built in the early 20th century with neoclassical and Renaissance features, it is worth a visit. It once belonged to the Secretariat of Communications and Transportation, and was donated to the National Museum of Art in the '80s. It has been fully restored and boasts beautiful hallways facing a central courtyard, columns with intricate details and – the pièce de résistance – a marble staircase right at the heart of the museum.

The museum's permanent collection is dedicated to Mexican works of art produced between the mid-16th century and the first half of the 20th century, and includes pieces by some of the greatest artists that the country has birthed, such as muralists David Alfaro Siqueiros and José Clemente Orozco, painter José Luis Cuevas (who actually belonged to the Rupturist Generation, which emerged in the mid-20th century to challenge the then-dominant Muralist Movement), photographer and communist activist Tina Modotti, and Saturnino Herrán, whose early 20th-century paintings portray Mexican Indigenous people with great strength and beauty.

The collection also includes sculpture, photography and decorative arts, and if navigating it sounds overwhelming, plan your visit between noon and 2pm, when the museum offers free guided tours (if you're with a group of five or more, email them beforehand to book a guide).

Tacuba 8, Centro
Histórico

Bellas Artes, lines 2
and 8; Allende, line 2
Bellas Artes, line 4

Tues–Sun 10am–6pm

$MXN
$70

W
munal.mx

Historic + Cultural Attractions

Museo del Templo Mayor

*Explore an archaeological site and walk among
the very origins of Mexico City.*

During the late 1970s and early '80s, archaeologist Eduardo Matos Moctezuma and his team unearthed the remains of Templo Mayor (the Aztec city of Tenochtitlan's Main Temple) in the very heart of Mexico City's historic centre. This pre-Hispanic site was once a large square plaza, with 78 buildings, including temples, altars and a ball-game court. It is considered the most important religious building in Tenochtitlan, as it was dedicated to Huitzilopochtli, god of the sun and war, and Tláloc, god of rain and agriculture.

    This major discovery not only included the building but also thousands of objects, which are currently displayed at the site museum, which is itself divided into eight galleries. These are based on the Temple's layout: the south side was dedicated to Huitzilopochtli – meaning that the first four galleries present war-related topics and items, while the north side was dedicated to Tláloc – making the last four galleries about agriculture and natural resources. In the main lobby, you'll find an enormous relief that honours Tlatecuhtli, goddess of the earth, which is believed to have been made in 1502. It was found in 2006, and has been painstakingly restored to its current state.

Seminario 8,
Centro Histórico

Zócalo, line 2
República de Argentina,
line 4

Tues–Sun 9am–5pm

$MXN

$75

W

templomayor.inah.gob.mx

Historic + Cultural Attractions

Antiguo Colegio de San Ildefonso

Murals of post-Revolution Mexico in a beautiful Baroque building.

Justo Sierra 16,
Centro Histórico

Allende, line 2
República de Argentina, line 4

Tues–Sun 10am–6pm

$MXN

$50, free on Sundays

W

sanildefonso.org.mx

San Ildefonso is known as the birthplace of the Mexican Muralist Movement, which emerged in the 1920s, thanks to a group of artists who sought to transmit their vision of the country's social and political situation. By painting murals, their goal was to educate the public through their art. This building is a beautiful work of architecture and it's lovely to walk around its hallways and courtyards. It began as a Jesuit institution in 1583, becoming one of the most important schools in Mexico. When the Jesuits were expelled from all Spanish territories in 1767, the building went through various incarnations, until, in 1992, it became a museum.

During its time as the National Preparatory School in the 1920s, the government commissioned several murals by masters: Diego Rivera, José Clemente Orozco, David Alfaro Siqueiros, Fermín Revueltas, Fernando Leal, Jean Chalot and Ramón Alva de la Canal. You can see Rivera's very first mural: *The Creation*, which he painted in 1922.

Museo Franz Mayer

Art, design and creativity in a building with a rich history.

Av. Hidalgo 45,
Centro Histórico

Bellas Artes, line 2
Bellas Artes, line 4

Tue–Sun 10am–5pm

$MXN

$60

W

franzmayer.org.mx

The beautiful 16th-century building was once a hospital and its rich history makes it the perfect home for this non-profit institution, founded by German collector and philanthropist Franz Mayer.

At the heart of the museum are exquisite items collected by Mayer: furniture, photographs, azulejo tiles, silverware, clocks, paintings, textiles and maps, spanning six centuries. Don't miss the Ruth D. Lechuga popular art collection, featuring colourful masks, toys and textiles, and a gorgeous collection of silver jewellery produced by William Spratling. The museum's lovely central courtyard, filled with flowers and a tranquil fountain, calls for a stroll before you head back out to the city's busy centre.

If you're in town during August and September, check out the World Press Photo exhibition.

Historic + Cultural Attractions

Palacio de Bellas Artes

A true icon of Mexico City.

This stunning white marble palace, home to the theatre and the Museum of Fine Arts, was commissioned by President Porfirio Díaz at the beginning of the 20th century, as part of his plans to bring beauty and grandeur to the capital. Italian architect Adamo Boari was in charge of the project, giving it its elegant Carrara marble exteriors and Art Nouveau touches. Construction was halted when the Revolution started in 1910; Mexican architect Federico Mariscal took over the project again in 1928, adding an Art Deco-style and using modern onyx and marble for the lobby and interiors; and in 1934, it finally opened its doors as the Palace of Fine Arts.

Inside, you'll find murals by some of Mexico's most influential artists, including José Clemente Orozco's *Catharsis*, David Alfaro Siqueiros' *The New Democracy*, Rufino Tamayo's *Mexico Today* and Diego Rivera's *Man at the Crossroads*. The museum also holds major temporary exhibitions, which in the past have included *Toulouse-Lautrec's Paris, Russian Vanguard* and *Leonardo Da Vinci and the Idea of Beauty*.

If you're lucky, you might catch a performance inside the theatre, so check the website and book your tickets before your visit. The National Symphony Orchestra and the Folkloric ballet frequently perform here, and the stage is crowned by a stained-glass curtain with a picture of the Popocatépetl and Iztaccíhuatl volcanoes by 20th-century landscape artist Dr Atl.

📍
Av. Juárez,
Centro Histórico

Bellas Artes, lines 2, 8
Bellas Artes, line 4

⊗
Tues–Sun 10am–5pm

$MXN
$70, free on Sundays

W
museopalaciodebellas
artes.gob.mx

Biblioteca Vasconcelos

*Hundreds of bookshelves
and a garden to read in.*

Eje 1 Norte, Buenavista

Buenavista, line B
Buenavista, lines 1, 3

Mon–Sun 8.30am–7.30pm

$MXN

free

W

bibliotecavasconcelos.gob.mx

With a mission to bring culture and education to everyone who wants it, this public library opened its doors in 2006. Architect Alberto Kalach created a building filled with open spaces and green areas. It holds 600,000 works, including books, magazines, newspapers, CDs and DVDs that can be borrowed or consulted on site.

Explore its many interesting rooms, including the music room and the children's area; head outside to the gardens, where you will find more than 168 types of plants and trees. The library frequently hosts cultural events, like chamber music concerts and educational workshops. It's also home to an intriguing work of art called *Mátrix Móvil* by plastic artist Gabriel Orozco, who took an 11-metre (36 feet) whale skeleton and transformed it into a hypnotising being that swims among the books.

Museo Memoria Y Tolerancia

Tolerance, human rights and respect for others.

Av. Juárez 8, Centro

Juárez, Line 3;
Bellas Artes, lines 2 and 8
Hidalgo, line 3

Tues–Fri 9am–6pm
Sat–Sun 10am–7pm

$MXN
$100, $120 with guide

W
myt.org.mx

This unique space opened its doors in 2010, with two permanent exhibitions: Memory and Tolerance. Memory is dedicated to the heinous 20th-century crimes against humanity, like the Holocaust and the Armenian genocide. The information is hard to digest but it sends a strong message linked to Tolerance. The pieces speak of the importance of dialogue, the power of the media, and highlight Mexico's rich and diverse cultural heritage, particularly of its Indigenous peoples. The exhibition finishes by showcasing social projects that aim to build a more equal society.

The museum also hosts temporary exhibitions, and an interactive area for children called Isla MYT Sésamo (in partnership with *Sesame Street*), encouraging values like tolerance and respect towards others' differences.

Plaza de la Constitución (Zócalo) & Catedral Metropolitana

Zócalo represents the beating heart of the city.

This massive square – Zócalo but officially called Plaza de la Constitución – isn't just big in size, but it frequently hosts all sorts of public events, from political rallies to concerts, and it is crowned by one of the 15 monumental Mexican flags in the country, which is raised every morning at 8am and is lowered at 6pm. You'll notice that locals come by to watch and be inspired by these ceremonies before going about their day. The square is surrounded by a variety of stores, restaurants and office buildings.

Zócalo is also flanked by buildings that tell the history of Mexico: Templo Mayor, the main Aztec temple in the city, built between the 15th and 16th centuries; the 16th-century Palacio Nacional, seat of the Federal Executive Power and home to the impressive mural the *Epic Poem of the Mexican People* by Diego Rivera; and Catedral Metropolitana, the majestic cathedral that was built over the course of almost three centuries. Its construction began in 1573 with the arrival of Hernán Cortés and the Spanish conquistadors and it was originally modelled after the Seville cathedral. Over time, gorgeous details were added, like the Baroque portals, the central panel featuring the Assumption of the Virgin Mary and the spectacular gilded Altar of the Kings behind the main altar. If you want to skip the crowds, the cathedral offers special night tours for small groups, as well as guided tours of the bell towers. You can purchase tickets through its website.

Plaza de la Constitución,
Centro Histórico

Zócalo, line 2
República de Argentina,
line 4

Mon–Sun 8am–8pm

$MXN
free

W
catedralmetropolitanacdmx.org

Historic + Cultural Attractions

Castillo de Chapultepec
(Museo Nacional de Historia)

*A castle and museum
dedicated to telling
the country's history.*

Bosque de Chapultepec,
1 Sección

Chapultepec, line 1;
Auditorio, line 7
Chapultepec, line 7

Tues–Sun 9am–5pm

$MXN

$75

W

mnh.inah.gob.mx

Sitting proudly atop Chapultepec Hill, this magnificent castle was built in 1785. It has been used as a summer house for Viceroy Bernardo de Gálvez, as a military academy, as the official residence of Emperor Maximilian I and his wife Carlota, and, then, official residence of the Mexican President. In 1939 it became home to the Museo Nacional de Historia.

The 12 halls will guide you through four centuries of Mexican history, from the encounter between two cultures during the period known as the New Spain, to the wars of Independence and Revolution, up until the birth of the Republic. There are re-creations of the rooms used by Maximilian and Carlota, as well as President Porfirio Díaz (known for his love of all things European). Highlights include Carlota's bedroom, with luxurious wallpapers and fabrics, and the dining room that Díaz commissioned from sculptor Pedro Téllez Toledo, with impressive wood and marble details.

Papalote Museo del Niño

A museum space where kids can learn through play.

Constituyentes 268,
Bosque de Chapultepec

Constituyentes, line 7

Mon–Wed & Fri 9am–6pm
Thurs 9am–6pm & 7pm–11pm
Sat–Sun 10am–7pm

$MXN

$199

W

papalote.org.mx

For more than 25 years, this museum has been a place of fun and discovery for kids of all ages under the motto: Touch, Play, and Learn. The colourful structure – visible from many parts of the city – houses interactive exhibitions that are divided into topics such as: My Body, My Home and My Family, My City, and the Idea Lab, all of which encourage children to learn through play.

Papalote (Spanish for kite), is also home to two high-tech entertainment venues: the ADO IMAX Megascreen and the Citibanamex Digital Dome, a screen made with 401 panels of aluminum and equipped with an impressive sound system, perfect for journeying to the ends of the universe.

Museo Nacional de Antropología

The legacy of Mesoamerica's pre-Hispanic people resides in this museum.

The main goal of this massive museum – the largest in the country – is honouring the history of Mexico's many Indigenous groups throughout the centuries and their legacy to the world. With 22 exhibition halls, it houses 5000 pieces that have been collected since 1790, when the sculpture of the Aztec earth goddess Coatlicue was found in the city's historic centre. Today, the museum features weapons, pottery, sculptures, textiles, jewellery and all sorts of items that give us a deeper understanding of the outstanding knowledge that pre-Hispanic cultures, like the Maya, the Zapotecas or the Toltecas, developed so many centuries ago. The centrepiece is the impressive Sun Stone, an intricately carved, 3.6-metre (11.8 feet), 25-tonne sculpture that was used for sacrifice.

The equally monumental building, developed by architect Pedro Ramírez Vázquez (in collaboration with Jorge Campuzano and Rafael Mijares) in 1964, includes a white marble facade that boasts the national coat of arms. The central patio is crowned by 'El Paraguas' (The Umbrella), a fountain with a bronze column sculpted by brothers, José and Tomás Chávez Morado. A recent addition is Sala Gastronómica, a beautiful restaurant in the heart of the museum that celebrates Mexican cuisine as another historic treasure to admire.

Paseo de la Reforma s/n,
Bosque de Chapultepec

Tues–Sun 9am–7pm

$MXN
$75

Auditorio, line 7
Antropología, line 7

W
mna.inah.gob.mx

Historic + Cultural Attractions

Museo Frida Kahlo

Frida Kahlo's former home is a must-visit.

To describe the cultural impact of Frida Kahlo, it's enough to see the lines outside this museum, also known as La Casa Azul. The sheer force of her personality and the endless controversy around her art have turned her into a role model for many. It's wise to buy your tickets through its website a few weeks in advance and, if possible, try to visit on a weekday to avoid the crowds.

As soon as you step inside, you'll understand that Frida's house makes perfect sense as a museum, as her art was always such an intimate reflection of her life. A victim of polio at the age of six and of a massive spinal injury at age 18, her story was always tainted with tragedy, but she was never afraid to address it in her work. Neither was she afraid of touching on themes like hope, her body and her great love for her husband, muralist Diego Rivera. Admire some of her most important paintings, like *Viva la Vida, My Family* and *Portrait of my Father Wilhem Kahlo,* as well as her favourite spaces, like her bedroom and the colourful kitchen. The gardens, filled with trees and plants, are a little oasis. If you love Frida Kahlo's work, also visit Museo Dolores Olmedo (see p.153).

Londres 247, Coyoacán

Tues & Thurs–Sun
10am–5.30pm
Wed 11am–5.30pm

$MXN
$256

W
museofridakahlo.org.mx

Historic + Cultural Attractions

Museo Soumaya

A modern marvel housing covetable collections.

A decade ago, a metallic, futuristic building emerged in a commercial area known as Nuevo Polanco, immediately capturing everyone's attention. Mexican architect Fernando Romero was in charge of creating this spaceship-like structure, completely covered with 16,000 hexagonal aluminum plaques that play with the sunlight throughout the day, creating all sorts of lovely visual effects as the hours go by.

The treasures found inside the museum are not quite as modern, yet are equally as appealing. Start your visit at the sixth level, The Rodin Era, home to the second-most important Auguste Rodin collection found outside France. Then walk down the ramp to continue your visit, which will lead you to find works by European masters from the 15th to the 18th centuries, such as Tintoretto and Rubens; Impressionist masterpieces from the likes of Monet and Degas; paintings, sculptures and houseware items from vice-regal times; and decorative arts in gold and silver.

Perhaps the main treat awaits at the very end, in the main lobby: there is a replica of Michelangelo's *Pietà*, as well as reproductions of Rodin's *Gates of Hell* and *The Thinker*, and Camille Claudel's *The Waltz*. Representing Mexico, you'll find Diego Rivera's last work, *Río Juchitán*, and two murals by Rufino Tamayo: *Still Life* and *Day and Night*.

Miguel de Cervantes
Saavedra 303, Granada
(Nuevo Polanco)

San Joaquín, line 7

Mon–Sun
10.30am–6.30pm

$MXN
free

W
museosoumaya.org

Xochimilco

Where nature meets history and folklore, while you sail along a canal.

Embarcadero Nativitas,
Calle del Mercado 133

Mon–Thurs 8am–7pm
Fri 8am–8.30pm
Sat 8am–10.30pm
Sun 8am–8pm

$MXN

$400–$2,000 (tours)

W

trajinerasxochimilco.com.mx

With more than 180 kilometres (111 miles) of waterways, you can sail Xochimilco's canals, while enjoying local food and a lively atmosphere. You'll see the centuries-old system of chinampas – artificial islands, used by the Aztecs to grow vegetables and flowers, and still used today. Your colourful boat, a trajinera, will be outfitted with a long table and some 20 seats, so it's bound to become a mobile party. Other trajineras around you offer food (like tacos and quesadillas), and you can even hire a trajinera carrying a mariachi band or a marimba player to sail alongside you.

The three most popular docks (which are also close to the plant and flower market) are: Nativitas, las Flores Nativitas and Zacapa, and it's best to book a tour online. If you'd like to visit the protected natural area, start your tour from the Fernando Celada, Cuemanco or Puente de Urrutia docks.

Museo Dolores Olmedo

Works by Kahlo, Rivera and other prominent Mexican artists.

Av. México 5843, Xochimilco

Tues–Sun 10am–6pm

$MXN

$100, free on Tuesdays

W

museodoloresolmedo.org.mx

The lovely 16th-century hacienda (estate) that houses this museum, called La Noria, once belonged to Dolores Olmedo, a businesswoman and philanthropist who during her lifetime donated her home and impressive art collection to the people of Mexico.

Olmedo was friends with Diego Rivera and Frida Kahlo, and the museum boasts the largest collection of the couple's work: more than 140 paintings by Rivera and more than 20 by Kahlo, plus some of her sketches. There are also engravings by Angelina Beloff, who was involved with Rivera during his stay in Europe, and Pablo O'Higgins, famous for depicting rural life in Mexico. Olmedo's collection includes more than 900 archaeological artifacts from pre-Hispanic times, and popular art from several states in Mexico, including blown glass and pottery.

The museum garden holds its own masterpieces, too. It's home to native trees, peacocks and hairless dogs called xoloitzcuintles, which are endemic to Mexico.

Historic + Cultural Attractions

Monumento a la Revolución (MRM)

A triumphal arch with a hidden story.

As the tallest triumphal arch in the world, at 67 metres (219 feet), the MRM celebrates the Mexican Revolution, and offers an amazing, 360-degree view of the city. It's hard to imagine that it hasn't always been standing proudly in the middle of Plaza de la República, but it hides a fascinating story inside its stone structure. A guided tour through architect Carlos Obregón Santacilia's building's 'soul of steel' will teach you about the technology used when construction began in 1910; how life was in Mexico at that time; and the decades of abandonment before its revival in 2010, for the Mexican Revolution centennial. Early birds shouldn't miss the chance to watch the city wake up from the very top of the monument – check the website for details on the Monumental Sunrise experience.

And if you're still hungry for more Revolution-related history, check out the Museo Nacional de la Revolución, located under Plaza de la República.

Plaza de la República, Tabacalera

Revolución, line 2
Plaza de la República, line 1

Mon–Thurs 12pm–8pm
Fri–Sat 12pm–10pm
Sun 10am–8pm

$MXN

Full access $90, limited access $60, Monumental Sunrise $400

W

mrm.mx

Historic + Cultural Attractions

Museo Nacional de San Carlos

One of the most important collections of European art in the country.

Spanish-born Manuel Tolsá was one of the most prolific architects of the 19th century, and this building is one of his most relevant pieces of work. The impressive neoclassical palace was once used as a private residence by prominent Mexican families, and was established as a museum in 1968 by the National Institute of Fine Arts.

It all began back in the 18th century, though, when the San Carlos Academy of the Arts began to form its collection, feeding it with work created by its very own students both here in Mexico and during their travels to Italy. Today the museum boasts pieces by masters like Parmigianino, Rodin, Van Dyck, Frans Hals and Tintoretto. The museum's Erik Larsen library is open to the public – just bring a valid ID – and offers more than 5000 books and magazines, including tomes dedicated to the plastic arts; the Primitivo Morales collection (focused on Mexico between 1900 and 1965); and the Erik Larsen collection, specialising in European art.

Puente de Alvarado 50, Tabacalera

Revolución, line 2
Museo San Carlos, line 4

Tues–Sun 10am–6pm

$MXN

$50, free on Sundays

W

mnsancarlos.inba.gob.mx

Historic + Cultural Attractions

MODERN + CONTEMPORARY ART

As you explore the city's modern and contemporary art scene, you'll immerse yourself in an ever-evolving landscape of creativity. Museums like Museo de Arte Moderno (see p.171) and Museo Tamayo (see p.173) will give you an excellent understanding of major moments and players in the country's art history, while pioneering galleries, such as kurimanzutto (see p.183) and OMR (see p.161), will inspire you to know more about the most groundbreaking artists – both local and international – in today's scene.

This chapter also guides you to museums that are masterpieces themselves, such as Museo Universitario Arte Contemporáneo (MUAC, see p.185) and Museo Jumex (see p.175). The impressive works of architecture are a confident announcement of what you'll find inside. And a bonus is that many of the galleries are free.

OMR

A 1960s brutalist home for contemporary art.

More than 30 years ago, partners Patricia Ortíz Monasterio and Jaime Riestra (who are also husband and wife) chose Plaza Río de Janeiro, one of the prettiest parks in the Roma neighbourhood, to open their gallery. Today, it's their son, Cristóbal Riestra, who is in charge of keeping the gallery as relevant as ever, now from its new home in one of the busiest areas in Roma Norte.

When this gallery opened, there was little – or nothing – happening in the city's contemporary art scene, and the groundbreaking project proved immediately influential. Ortíz Monasterio and Riestra started representing local and foreign artists – not only showing their art locally, but participating in international fairs as well. Today, the gallery's artist line-up ranges from international heavy-hitters, like American James Turrell (known for his work with light and space) and German photographer Candida Höfer, to Mexican rising stars, like sculptor Jose Dávila and multimedia and performance artist Pia Camil.

The current space boasts high ceilings, powerful concrete columns and an open floorplan that poses a new challenge for the artists, while offering them an exciting canvas to work with. The space allows them to experiment with everything from large-format photography to murals to installations that hang from the ceiling.

Córdoba 100, Roma Norte

Cuauhtémoc, line 1; Niños
Héroes, line 3
Jardín Pushkin, line 3

Tues–Thurs 10am–7pm
Fri 10am–4pm
Sat 11am–4pm

$MXN

Free

W

galeriaomr.com

Modern + Contemporary Art

Ángulo Cero

*Find unique pieces by artists and designers
at this gallery and design shop.*

From the beginning, this art gallery-meets-design store was born as an exhibition space for Mexican and Latin American designers living in Mexico, a place where they could sell their pieces and put their creative process on display. Today, although it has become a more formal establishment, it continues to promote art and design collections in Mexico, and to help local talent gain an international presence.

The more than 30 creators who work with Ángulo Cero, including experimental artist Fernando Laposse and Ad Hoc furniture studio, create unique or limited-edition pieces for the gallery, meaning each time you visit it's an exciting quest for a new find – be it a shelf, a rug, a lamp or a more travel-friendly piece of jewellery. Many of these – particularly furniture and houseware items – can be customised to your taste and can also be shipped internationally.

Ángulo Cero also has a corner at El Bazaar Sábado (see p.207), the popular crafts market in San Ángel, so make sure to pay a visit if you're there.

Chihuahua 56, 2nd floor,
Roma Norte

Niños Héroes, line 3
Jardín Pushkin, line 3

Mon–Fri 11am–7pm
Sat by appointment only

$MXN
Free

W
anguloo.com

Modern + Contemporary Art

Museo del Objeto del Objeto (MODO)

This quirky museum tells stories through design and curious objects.

Set in a gorgeous 1906 Art Nouveau house in the heart of Colonia Roma, MODO – short for Museo del Objeto del Objeto, or Museum of the Object of the Object – is a paradise for design lovers. It will be fascinating too, if you're interested in exploring culture through everyday items and knick-knacks, from photos and street signs to ads and toys.

The mastermind behind this project is founder Bruno Newman, who started collecting curious and rare objects over 40 years ago. Today, the museum's archive features more than 100,000 items, ranging from 1810 to our time, allowing it to present all sorts of themed temporary exhibitions that offer a fresh point of view of Mexico's history. Past exhibitions have explored topics such as Rock in Mexico, Lucha Libre – Mexican-style wrestling – and kitchen utensils.

You should definitely visit the giftshop. Notebooks, coffee mugs, books and jewellery are some of the original items you can take home.

Colima 145, Roma Norte

Tues–Sun 10am–6pm

$MXN

$50

Niños Héroes, line 3
Jardín Pushkin, line 3

W

elmodo.mx

Modern + Contemporary Art

PROYECTOSMONCLOVA

Carefully selected contemporary art by multi-generational artists from Mexico and abroad.

The first thing you'll probably notice when you step inside this Roma neighbourhood gallery is the lovely vertical garden to your left, which seems fitting for a space that's all about letting ideas and art grow freely. Born in 2005, PROYECTOSMONCLOVA is a team effort by partners Teófilo Cohen and David Trabulsi with gallery director Polina Stroganova, who joined forces with them after having worked in London and Berlin.

When it comes to the 15 artists under the gallery's representation, it's an eclectic yet carefully selected mix. More than half of them are Mexican, like multidisciplinary artists Chantal Peñalosa and Eduardo Terrazas, while others hail from Germany (sculptor Michael Sailstorfer) and Slovenia (sculptor and performance artist Ištvan Išt Huzjan). They cover different generations as well – Peñalosa was born in the 1980s, while veteran Terrazas was born in 1936. What they all have in common is a way of working that the gallery owners can relate to, as well as an original message to communicate. The curation behind this is that it should not just be about the artist displaying new work, but about them having something new and meaningful to say. This means that the exhibitions (between eight and 10 each year) are always worth checking out, whether they're showcasing an individual artist or a specific topic.

Colima 55, Roma Norte

Niños Héroes, line 3
Jardín Pushkin, line 3

Tues–Fri 10am–6pm
Sat 11am–4pm

$MXN

Free

W

proyectosmonclova.com

Modern + Contemporary Art

Galería López Quiroga

*An incredible landscape of modern art
and artists in Latin America.*

The list of artists represented by this prestigious gallery reads like a who's who of modern and contemporary art in Mexico and Latin America. Its reputation for showcasing the best talent is an honour that has been well earned over a four-decade trajectory. Local painters and sculptors portray a glorious landscape of how art has developed in the region over the past years. Here you'll see work by artists like Pedro Coronel, Vicente Rojo, Irma Palacios, Francisco Toledo, Manuel Felguérez, Miguel Castro Leñero and Rufino Tamayo, and photographers such as Graciela Iturbide, Lola and Manuel Álvarez Bravo, Guillermo Kahlo, Héctor García, Lázaro Blanco and Sebastião Salgado. If some of these names don't ring a bell, a quick online research session before your visit will help you see how they helped to shaped the course of Latin American modern art.

Throughout the gallery's history, owner Ramón López Quiroga has focused his efforts on his home base, instead of having presence at local and international art fairs. The gallery also publishes specialised books and catalogues to further promote its artists' work, and it presents between four and six exhibitions each year, either dedicated to individual artists or a theme.

The beautiful space (a two-level house in the heart of Polanco) not only serves as a great space for the artwork, but also features a large display window that faces the street and draws curious neighbours from the area to come a little closer and enjoy a taste of the art on their way home.

Horacio 714, Polanco

Mon–Fri 10am–7pm
Sat 10am–2pm

$MXN

Free

🚌

Polanco, line 7

W

lopezquiroga.com

Modern + Contemporary Art

Museo de Arte Moderno

*A great archive of Mexican modern art resides
in this interesting building.*

With more than 3000 paintings, sculptures, drawings, and photographs, this museum holds one of the largest archives of 20th-century Mexican art. It boasts work from Muralists like José Clemente Orozco, Diego Rivera, and David Alfaro Siqueiros; and the artists whose movement, the Rupture, followed them, such as Pedro Coronel and Manuel Felguérez. It also features photographs from Manuel Álvarez Bravo – one of the most recognised photographers in the country – and a large collection of sculptures and paintings from surrealist Remedios Varo. Head to Halls C and D, located on the ground floor of the main building, to delve into the fascinating permanent collection.

A symbol of Mexico's entrance to the modern age, the museum was built by architect Pedro Ramírez Vázquez in 1964, a creation of marble, fibreglass and aluminium. The five domes in its two buildings have a peculiar feature: they are sound amplifiers. The museum has taken advantage of this by developing Bosque Sonoro (Loud Forest), a series of experimental music performances. Make sure to check its website in advance – you might just catch one during your visit.

There is plenty to enjoy outside the galleries, too. Its cafeteria, Irracional Café, not only brews great cups of coffee but also offers picnic food and tea tastings in the museum's sculpture garden.

Paseo de la Reforma
and Gandhi, Bosque de
Chapultepec

Tues–Sun
10.15am–5.30pm

$MXN

$70

W

mam.inba.gob.mx

Chapultepec, line 1
Gandhi, line 7

Modern + Contemporary Art

Museo Tamayo

*Artist Rufino Tamayo's legacy lives
on at this influential museum.*

Oaxacan painter Rufino Tamayo, one of the most influential and beloved artists in Mexico, founded this museum in 1981, a decade before he passed away. His work is at the heart of the museum, whose mission is to showcase the most innovative pieces of modern and contemporary art. The legacy of Tamayo and his wife, Olga, resonates through both through its permanent collection and its temporary exhibitions. The modern art collection is a summary of the Avant Garde movements of the late 20th century, while the contemporary art collection, curated after Tamayo's passing, aims to bring continuity to his vision, and each piece has either been donated or created exclusively for the museum by the artist. Past temporary exhibition highlights include Yayoi Kusama's Infinite Obsession and Noguchi's Parks.

The building, which blends into the surrounding Chapultepec landscape, was designed by Mexican architects Teodoro González de León and Abraham Zabludovsky. Because of the way that it seems to sprout from the ground and how it allows for a clever interaction of light and shadow, it's not only an interesting sight for visitors, but it earned its designers a National Arts and Sciences Award in 1982.

For a further taste of Mexican creativity, you should make a stop at the store – focused on local design – and the restaurant, which specialises in contemporary Mexican food. And remember to take a look at the museum's website before your visit. You can book a guided tour in English, or perhaps book one of their movie or live jazz nights.

Paseo de la Reforma 51,
Bosque de Chapultepec

Chapultepec, line 1
Gandhi, line 7

Tues–Sun 10am–6pm;
open until 9.30pm on
the last Wednesday of
the month

$MXN

$70,
free on Sundays

W

museotamayo.org

Modern + Contemporary Art

Museo Jumex

*A strong contemporary art collection and exciting
temporary exhibitions.*

One of the city's newest offerings, this museum opened its doors at the end
of 2013, a layered building designed by British architect David Chipperfield.
The goal: to bring contemporary art to a wider audience and to provide
artists with a space in which to experiment freely. Founder Eugenio López
Alonso, one of the most prominent collectors of contemporary art in the
country, created a non-profit art foundation in 2001 (Fundación Jumex Arte
Contemporáneo), and this museum is the confirmation of his legacy.

The ground floor is an open, welcoming space that connects the
museum to the city, while the next three levels feature terraces and skylights
that allow the outside light to interact with the interiors. Throughout its short
yet prolific history, the museum has already hosted several major successful
exhibitions, so you can expect to see iconic works. Past exhibitions include:
Andy Warhol, Dark Star (2017), *Appearance Stripped Bare: Desire and the
Object in the Work of Marcel Duchamp* and *Jeff Koons, Even* (2019). It also
boasts a strong permanent collection, featuring work by some of the most
relevant contemporary artists in Mexico, such as Pedro Reyes, Abraham
Cruzvillegas, and Minerva Cuevas plus international names like Mike Kelley
and Roni Horn (USA).

To top it all off, the onsite cafe is an outpost of Eno, famed chef Enrique
Olvera's (see p.88 and 93) casual eatery. If you're interested in booking a
guided tour in English, email grupos@fundacionjumex.org a few days
in advance.

📍
Blvd Miguel de Cervantes
Saavedra 303, Granada,
Nuevo Polanco

🕗
Tues–Sun 10am–7pm

$MXN
$50

🚇
San Joaquín/Polanco,
line 7

W
fundacionjumex.org

Modern + Contemporary Art

Galería Ethra

*A former factory becomes a home for local
and international plastic artists.*

The story of this gallery finds its origins way back when its founders, Andrea Walther and Rodrigo Borrás, were in their teens. They had the chance to see many projects that sought to bring art to Mexico from up close, and fell in love with the scene then. In 2008, they opened the doors to their project in the Colonia Juárez neighbourhood, hoping to contribute to the development of plastic arts – all those that produce work are meant to be viewed and admired in Mexico and the world. Eleven years later, they made a bold move, finding a new location in a former factory in the Nuevo Polanco area. This new open space invites artists to get more involved in the area. With their new home comes a new feature: each year, an artist is invited to take up residency in the gallery.

Today, there are 15 national and international artists under the gallery's representation. Local talent includes Pedro Friedeberg, a designer and artist known for his surrealist work, and María José de la Macorra, whose work is based on the beauty of plants. On the international front, there are names like Jae-Hyo Lee, a South Korean artist who turns discarded pieces of wood into stunning pieces.

Lago Texcoco 112 B-Bis,
Anáhuac 1 Sección,
Nuevo Polanco

Colegio Militar, line 2

Mon–Fri 10am–7pm
Sat 11am–3pm

$MXN

Free

W

galeriaethra.com

Arredondo\Arozarena

*A platform for up-and-coming artists
in the heart of the city.*

If you're walking around the eclectic streets of the city's downtown area, chances are you might see an intriguing shop window that stands out from the rest of the businesses that surround it. Among old-school stationery stores and dentist offices stands this young yet reputable contemporary art gallery. It partly owes its success to its Proyecto Vitrina, which translates as 'shop window project': displaying art for any passer-by to enjoy, and trying to challenge the often intimidating concept of the closed-doors gallery.

 The gallery was opened by Andrés Arredondo in 2010 and a few years later he teamed up with his wife, Georgina Arozarena, to further develop the project. One of the risks they chose to take was to leave the gallery's former home – a 1930s house in Colonia Juárez, a more commercial neighbourhood – and move right to the heart of the city, offering their artists an entirely different area in which to work. But in spite of all the changes, the gallery's main goal remains the same: to promote young, up-and-coming artists – like multidisciplinary artists Israel Martínez, from Mexico, and Marilá Dardot, from Brazil – whose work will make you question who we are as a society.

 Fun fact: on Saturdays, a traditional market sets up right outside the gallery, where you can find fresh cheeses, breads, and all sorts of street snacks.

Ezequiel Montes 36,
Tabacalera

Hidalgo, line 2
Hidalgo, line 4

Tues–Fri 10am–6pm
Sat 11am–3pm

$MXN
Free

W
arredondoarozarena.com

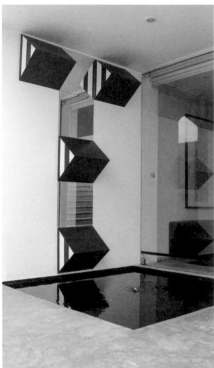

Galería Hilario Galguera

*Contemporary art set in a lovely mansion
from the early 20th century.*

While this gallery is located in one of the oldest neighbourhoods in the city, Colonia San Rafael, and set inside a beautiful house from the Porfirian era – the beginning of the 20th century – once you step inside, the space becomes decidedly current: it's all about contemporary art. This gallery owes its conception to none other than British artist Damien Hirst. Legend has it that it was Hirst who convinced owner Hilario Galguera to start this project back in 2006; after putting together the artist's first Latin American show, Galguera has continued to represent him in Mexico.

The gallery has always been committed to both introducing established artists – like French conceptual artist Daniel Buren – to local audiences, and helping develop the careers of Mexican artists. Painter Bosco Sodi and sculptor Benjamín Torres, for example, have grown alongside the gallery and are now two of the most respected names in the contemporary art scene.

The house's layout makes for an interesting experience, as there are not only several exhibition rooms, but also a lovely courtyard with a small fountain. Get lost among the artwork and end your visit with a stop in the bookstore – a clever set of shelves offering specialised magazines and books, some of them published by the gallery.

Francisco Pimentel 3,
San Rafael

San Cosme, Revolución,
line 1
Revolución, line 1

Mon–Thurs
10am–5.30pm
Friday 11am–2pm

$MXN

Free

W

galeriahilariogalguera.com

kurimanzutto

*One of the most influential contemporary
art galleries in the country.*

It's impossible to talk about contemporary art galleries in Mexico City without mentioning kurimanzutto. Born in 1999, the project started out as a roving gallery, when Mexican artist Gabriel Orozco encouraged founders Mónica Manzutto and José Kuri – a couple of art dealers (who also happen to be married) – to support local creators. At the time, galleries and contemporary art museums were scarce in the country and the duo stepped into the scene at the right moment, teaming up with 14 artists for their initial line-up.

It wasn't until 2008 that the gallery found its current home in the tree-lined streets of San Miguel Chapultepec, a residential area that is just steps away from Condesa and Bosque de Chapultepec. The building, which once served as a lumberyard and later as a bakery, was transformed by renowned architect Alberto Kalach into a bright, airy exhibition space, with large wooden beams that honour the space's past, and allows for plenty of natural light to come in and bathe the artwork.

Today, the gallery represents more than 30 of the most widely recognised names in the contemporary art world, both from Mexico – such as conceptual artist Minerva Cuevas and multidisciplinary artist Mariana Castillo Deball – and abroad, like Argentinian sculptor Adrián Villar Rojas and Albanian Anri Sala, who works with video and photographs.

Rafael Rebollar 94,
San Miguel Chapultepec

Juanacatlán, line 1;
Constituyentes, line 7
Parque Lira, line 2

Tues–Thurs 11am–6pm
Fri–Sat 11am–4pm

$MXN

Free

W

kurimanzutto.com

Museo Universitario Arte Contemporáneo (MUAC)

*The first museum in the country dedicated
to contemporary art.*

The sprawling UNAM (National Autonomous University of Mexico) campus is home to this museum, MUAC, housed in a modernist building by famed Mexican architect Teodoro González de León. Opened in 2008, it was the first one in the country to be dedicated entirely to contemporary art, and its collection boasts pieces from 1952 – the year that the university was founded – and focuses mostly on national art, featuring names like Vicente Rojo and Abraham Cruzvillegas. The museum has also partnered with particular collections, further enriching its landscape.

Aside from its impressive history of temporary exhibitions – it has hosted major names, like Zaha Hadid Architects, Ai Weiwei, Yves Klein, Lance Wyman, Anish Kapoor and Jan Hendrix – MUAC is also known for its educational efforts. It frequently hosts workshops and talks that encourage visitors of all ages to interact with its collection and exhibitions, and its specialised library features more than 4000 books on modern and contemporary art.

On the ground floor, you'll find Nube Siete, a contemporary Mexican restaurant serving breakfast and lunch with a lovely view of the university's ecological reserve. You'll also discover the museum shop, offering a selection of design-centred items like jewellery, furniture, clothing and books – many of which can only be found here, plus incredibly cool toys for kids.

Insurgentes 3000,
Ciudad Universitaria

/

Universidad, line 3
Centro Cultural
Universitario, line 1

Wed, Fri & Sun
10am–6pm
Thurs & Sat 10am–8pm

$MXN

$40
Wed & Sun: $20
Thurs & Sat: free entrance
6–8pm

W

muac.unam.mx

MARKETS + SHOPS

Shopping is a fantastic way to connect with Mexico City – to understand its people, their creativity, their aesthetics and their stories. The ultimate goal is for you to go back home with beautiful, unique items that will always remind you of this city. This chapter includes stores that showcase Mexico's current bustling creative scene, such as maker Carla Fernández (see p. 194) creating traditional Mexican textiles with a contemporary twist, and Sofía Álvarez's brand Libélula (see p. 196), with original Mexican jewellery designs.

This chapter also takes you to five of the city's most exciting markets. Markets are deeply embedded in our culture and this selection will give you a taste of the things we enjoy the most – namely food, flowers and art. For food, browse the stalls at Mercado San Juan (see p. 193); you'll find flowers in every form and colour at Mercado Jamaica (see p. 209); and La Ciudadela (see p. 191) is your art destination for crafts from all over the country. We haven't included a price guide for markets (only for shops), as you might get a tiny little craft piece for 20 pesos and then find some crazy sculpture for 40,000 pesos!

Escópica

A family-run eyewear shop with an excellent selection and personalised service.

Shopping for eyewear – and having your eyes checked – has never been as enjoyable as it is at this beautiful family owned store. Brothers Diego and Javier Graue personally choose the brands that are on display here, searching for top quality and design. The excellent selection features international brands, such as Eyevan7285 (Japan), Moscot (the United States), Karmoie (Norway), and Cutler and Gross (United Kingdom), which sit alongside Gramo, the house brand (produced in Japan), and antique finds from around the world.

The beautifully displayed glasses and sunglasses make it a treat to browse but so does the store itself: the space is filled with natural light and boasts exposed brick walls, large mirrors and comfortable chairs.

To ensure that you leave with exactly the pair of glasses you want, you are welcome to sit down, have a cup of coffee, and try as many pairs as you like. Also, eye exams and customised lenses are part of the deal, as are full repair services, which take between three and seven days so that you can have it done while you're in Mexico City. The shop also offers international shipments, in case your stay is a bit shorter. And if you like what you're listening to in-store, you can check out the playlist of the month on its website.

Colima 138, Roma Norte

Niños Héroes, line 3
Jardín Pushkin, line 3

Mon–Sat 11am–8pm
Sun 11am–6pm

$MXN

$1900–$12,000

W

escopica.com

Viriathus

Get lost among antiques and unique items – all with a story.

Mérida 10, Roma Norte

Cuauhtémoc, Insurgentes, line 1
Glorieta Insurgentes, line 1

Mon–Fri 9am–7pm
Sat 11am–6pm

$MXN

prices vary

W

viriathus.com.mx

The past comes alive at this quirky antiques store, founded by a pair of brothers with a passion for history. It all began innocently enough, when Ernesto Viriato Cuenca, an art historian, started collecting curious antiques, until he didn't have any room in his house to store them. His brother, Viriato – yes, they share a name – suggested they turn his hobby into a business and that's how the store came to be. Their philosophy has been to find objects that have a story to tell and will become timeless in your home.

The store, with its many rooms to explore, is the perfect space for you to travel in time. You'll discover old photographs and manuscripts, lamps and chandeliers, first edition books and gorgeous pieces of furniture, like desks and chairs from the early 20th century. Most items come with a detailed fact-sheet explaining where and when they come from. Take note that the store does not offer international shipments, so if you purchase a large item, you're in charge of its journey to your destination.

La Ciudadela

A lovely market offering arts and crafts from all over Mexico.

Balderas s/n, Centro Histórico

Juárez, line 3; Balderas, lines 1, 3
Juárez, line 3

Mon–Sat 10am–7pm
Sun 10am–6pm

W

laciudadela.com.mx

Colourful, elaborate and impossibly charming, Mexican crafts tell stories; and getting lost in this maze of a market is a wonderful way to understand the range of the country's creations. Its history can be traced back to the 1968 Olympics, when the government asked artisans from all over the country to display their work. Two years later, during the soccer World Cup, the place also served as a handcraft hotspot and its success hasn't wavered since.

There are more than 300 stalls but it's easy to navigate, so take your time and compare prices, as many vendors offer similar items. Admire fantastic alebrijes (wooden sculptures of fantastical creatures) from Oaxaca, silver jewellery, textiles in all shapes and sizes – from rugs to hammocks to huipil blouses and dresses (traditional embroidered garments worn and made by Indigenous women), intricate Olinalá trays, Huichol sculptures decorated with beads, and fun, kitschier items, like lucha libre masks and T-shirts. Several vendors take credit cards but it's easier bringing cash.

Markets + Shops

Mercado San Juan

From unusual meats to fresh vegetables,
this market is a gourmet paradise.

If there's one thing you're going to need at this market, It's an appetite. Beloved by chefs and food lovers from in and out of town, this is the place for high-quality ingredients, from bright, ripe fruit to crazy-sounding stuff, like alligator meat (really). The best course of action is just to walk around and ask for samples whenever possible.

Fruit and vegetable vendors carefully assemble the freshest limes, mangos, bananas and harder-to-find items, like passionfruit or yucca. At the seafood section, you'll spot heaps of shrimp and huge snappers so fresh that it might feel like they're looking at you; butchers and poulterers will be minding their own business, usually to the sound of loud music; the meat vendors at Los Coyotes will ask if you're interested in trying some deer, rabbit, bison, armadillo or do you care for an ostrich taco?; and at La Jersey (my personal favourite), a small glass of clericot will convince you to have a seat and order a baguette filled with fantastic cold cuts and cheeses from Italy and Spain. You won't be sorry. Deal with the post-lunch yawns with a cup of coffee from Triana Café, with beans that hail from Veracruz.

Segunda Calle de Ernesto
Pugibet 21, Centro

Mon–Sun 9am–5pm

San Juan de Letrán, line 8
Plaza San Juan, line 4

Carla Fernández

*Traditional Mexican
textiles meet modern,
daring design.*

_____

Marsella 72, Juárez

Cuauhtémoc, line 1
Glorieta Insurgentes, line 1

Mon–Sat 10am–8pm
Sun 9am–7pm

$MXN

$1,000–$15,000

W

carlafernandez.com

Designer Carla Fernández honours the centuries-old tradition of creating intricate and colourful Mexican textiles by working closely with artisans from states like Yucatán, Puebla and Chiapas. The result: avant-garde pieces that preserve heritage. The modern, geometric shapes of her shirts, coats and ponchos and the detailed embroidery, make for a unique combination; and she's never afraid to challenge the traditional way that a skirt or a dress is worn.

Her flagship store opened in 2019. The house was designed by her husband, renowned artist and sculptor Pedro Reyes, and it's a feast for the eyes. The ground floor of women's clothing features a stunning pre-Hispanic tiled floor, while the first level, showing menswear, looks more like a modern art museum than a store. The second floor is used for special events and workshops.

You will also find other brands who share her ethical fashion philosophy, such as hammocks by Angela Damman, sandals by Yolotli and jewellery by Varon Studio.

Loose Blues

Japanese-inspired threads and a selection of vintage finds.

Dinamarca 44, Juárez

Cuauhtémoc, line 1
Glorieta Insurgentes, line 1

Tues–Sat 9am–10.30pm
Sun 9am–7pm

$MXN

$1500–$16,000

The beauty and balance of Japanese aesthetics with a rebellious vintage touch inspires this peculiar shop. Owners Shota Kimura and Jacqueline Mota personally choose the brands and pieces that you'll find here.

The men's section is inspired by tattoo and motorcycle culture, and features Japanese brands like The Softmachine, known for their cool graphic T-shirts, and Rwche, whose hats, socks and hoodies mix design with a sense of humour. In the women's section, don't miss the chunky sweaters and wide-leg pants by Todayful (also hailing from Japan). The shelves boast jewellery by Mexican designer Michaela González, who works with silver and semi-precious stones and gorgeous leather handbags and wallets by Robin Archives.

Head upstairs for quirky vintage pieces, from desks and chairs to vinyl records and kitchenware. Plus there's a dining room that serves a casual international menu that changes constantly. The space also hosts interesting events, like art exhibitions and tattoo sessions.

Libélula

Creative jewellery inspired by nature.

Liverpool 76, Juárez

Cuauhtémoc, line 1
Hamburgo, line 1

Open by appointment

$MXN

$1,000 but prices vary
for custom-made pieces

W

libelulaporsofia.com

Nature is a source of inspiration for Sofía Álvarez, founder of this 100% Mexican jewellery brand. After all, it's not a coincidence that libélula means firefly. Sofía is a certified gemologist and over the past decade she has let her imagination and creativity fly, developing themed collections such as Tierra, with roots and branches as its main elements, and Stag Beetle, where the friendly bug sits on top of rings and earrings.

The brand has also expanded with collections for men, with chunky rings and cuffs; and Atelier, one-of-a-kind pieces made upon request with precious stones like emeralds, aquamarines and sapphires. There's also a super-cute line called Básicos of everyday rings, necklaces and bracelets. And for those looking for a unique engagement ring, Sofía will work closely with you throughout the process.

To visit the showroom, located in a house in Colonia Juárez, contact beforehand to make an appointment.

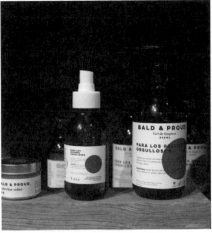

Casa Caballería

Clothes, accessories and grooming items for the modern man.

Havre 64, Juárez

Cuauhtémoc, line 1
Hamburgo, line 1

Mon–Sat 11am–8pm
Sun 11am–6pm

$MXN
Average item $3000

W
casacaballeria.com

A true paradise for gentlemen, this multi-level house has gained a cult following in the city since it opened in 2014. It gives space to up-and-coming designers to showcase their creations. You'll find around 120 Mexican brands, including Pay's (colourful knitwear), 1/8 Takamura (Japanese-inspired clothes) and their own line, Caballería (impeccably made shoes). There are also brands from Peru, Colombia and Catalonia that might be hard to find elsewhere, and the constant rotation makes each visit a treat.

You'll also find grooming products – the Mr. Man line for beards and the innovative Bald and Proud products, as well as books, accessories, kitchenware and leather goods from Mexican brands like Mr. Fox and Miles & Louie.

And don't miss a stop at the Denim Lab. Choose everything from the denim (Mexican or Japanese) to the zipper and pockets and, if your travels allow for it, come back in 10 business days for jeans made just for you.

Markets + Shops

Casa Salt

Quirky and cute rule this inspiring design shop.

At Casa Salt, love becomes design and browsing around this adorable shop is guaranteed to make you smile. The mastermind behind this project is Valeria Salt, the designer behind Salt & Tenorio, who started her brand in 2013. This inspired her to create a larger platform where Mexican designers she knew and loved could share their work. Here, Valeria showcases brands and items that she'd like to find herself, which means you'll be looking for a little something for your friends but end up buying something for yourself.

Explore treasures like tiny animal-shaped plant pots by Maceleo, delicate jewellery by Minimal, cute pins by Jedzilla – among the house's top-selling items – essential oils and aromatherapy sprays by Aroma 72 (with cheeky names like Namasté Bitches) and notebooks by illustrator Sofía Weidner, among many others. What all brands share, explains Valeria, is that they're fun, modern and emotional.

From time to time, Casa Salt hosts pop-up events, such as tattoo parties, which are always a big hit. They also have an outpost downtown, inside Barrio Alameda cultural and shopping centre and you'll find mostly the same selection at both locations.

Juan de la Barrera and
Pachuca, Condesa

Mon–Sun 11am–8pm

$MXN
$30–$3000

Chapultepec, line 1
Sonora, line 1

Mercado Medellín

*A destination for gourmet items and
Latin American products.*

While smaller in scale than other markets in the city, Medellín's location and friendly size make it a great option if you want a taste of the public market experience: good food, colourful piñatas, fresh flowers and quirky toys. You're bound to find plenty of locals shopping for fresh fruits and vegetables, canned goods, cold cuts and other deli items, but it's particularly popular because of the abundance of Latin American products. Flags from Colombia, Venezuela and Honduras announce the presence of all sorts of goodies brought from southern territories. You may find fresh produce, like yams, yucca and lulo (a tropical fruit), and products like Inca Kola soda from Peru, Bustelo coffee from Cuba, and Milo, a popular chocolate powder.

Whatever you do, make sure you stop at Helados Palmeiro, the ice-cream corner run by the incredibly charming Eugenio Palmeiro. 'Once you've tried Cuban ice-cream, you'll be back at least once a month,' he promises as soon as you sit down. And he's not wrong. The flavour choice includes options like mamey, coconut, tangerine and the very popular nata (thick cream), served with a side of friendly chatter.

Campeche 101, Condesa   Mon–Sun 8.30am–6pm

Chilpancingo, line 9
Chilpancingo, line 1

Ikal

A carefully curated concept store where creativity rules.

Presidente Masaryk
340A, Polanco

Polanco, line 7

Mon–Sat 11am–8pm
Sun 12pm–6pm

$MXN

$300–$16,000

W

ikalstore.com

Located on the city's prime shopping street, Presidente Masaryk, this concept store is inspired by teamwork, as its founders firmly believe that the artists and designers whose work is on display benefit from each other's creativity. Thus the name Ikal, which is Maya for 'in search for the spirit'. There are more than 70 national and international brands coexisting here.

The store is divided into easily browsable sections: womenswear, menswear, accessories, skincare, books, art and design. Some of the coolest Mexican brands you will find here are Anndra Neen – sisters who design unique jewellery; Ayres – gorgeous kitchenware, like wooden trays and modern stone molcajetes (traditional tools for making salsa); For all Folks – unisex body-care items; and Maison Manila – updated classic fashion for men and women. An especially beloved brand is Mr. Fox, whose leather handbags, wallets and travel notebooks have a beautiful, timeless look. International standouts include sunglasses makers Bob Sdrunk and bags and briefcases from The Bridge (both Italian brands).

El Péndulo

A bookstore and coffee shop with live music and a welcoming atmosphere.

Alejandro Dumas 81, Polanco

Polanco, line 7

Mon & Wed 8am–11pm
Thurs & Fri 8am–12am
Sat 9am–11pm
Sun 9am–10pm

$MXN

$70–$3000

W

pendulo.com

For those who are feeling a bit despondent about the future of books or good old human interaction in the digital age, this bookstore-meets-restaurant is a nice reminder that everything's not lost. For almost three decades, El Péndulo (with six locations across town, all of them equally welcoming) has provided readers with endless material, from new releases and bestsellers to tomes on art, design, film, photography and poetry, among many other topics. There is also a wide selection of CDs and DVDs, including everything from hit TV shows to documentaries and films from around the world. You can also browse around for toys, stationery and memorabilia. At the restaurant, you'll find unpretentious dishes – pancakes, enchiladas and omelettes at breakfast; salads, sandwiches and pasta dishes at lunch and dinner – and a generally relaxed atmosphere.

On Saturdays, breakfasts come with a side of live music, while on many evenings, you'll encounter events like readings or music performances.

Mercado Coyoacán

With everything from fresh produce to authentic
crafts, this market is one of the most popular in town.

Located in the very heart of the colourful neighbourhood of Coyoacán, this market was founded in 1921, but moved to its current, larger location in 1956. It's one of the most popular markets in the city, as it holds a world of folklore within its walls. While it occupies an entire block, the layout – with three main aisles – makes it quite easy to navigate. Find traditional crafts, like embroidered huipil dresses and blouses and adorable María dolls from the state of Querétaro; festive piñatas shaped like stars, animals or movie characters; and kids' costumes for all occasions. The market is particularly fun to visit during holidays, like Día de Muertos (our celebration of the Day of the Dead, held on 1 and 2 November), Independence Day (16 September), or Christmas, when you'll find all sorts of decorations.

If you have an esoteric interest, you will be delighted to explore stall 227, run by a lady named Chela, who not only sells an impressive array of candles, incenses and herbs, but also offers readings and other mystical services. And you don't want to miss the market's snack par excellence: the legendary Tostadas Coyoacán. Simple yet delicious, the tostadas can be topped with shrimp, crab, chicken or meat. Add a bit of salsa or sour cream and you'll have enough energy to keep shopping for hours.

Finally, keep in mind that most vendors don't like it when you photograph their stalls and they will charge you two dollars per photo.

Ignacio Allende s/n,
Del Carmen, Coyoacán

Mon–Sun 8.30am–6pm

W
centrodecoyoacan.mx

Coyoacán, line 3

Markets + Shops

LoredAna

Grooming products made with natural and organic ingredients.

Calle de la Amargura 5,
San Ángel

Bombilla, line 1

Mon–Thurs 11.30am–7.30pm
Fri 11am–7.30pm
Sat 11am–8pm
Sun 11am–7pm

$MXN

$100–$300

W

loredana.mx

This pretty space brings to mind an old apothecary shop with a chic touch. Mexico has a long tradition of botanical sciences and for centuries the country's natural resources have been used to cure diseases and improve health. The urge to recover this knowledge is the motivation behind LoredAna, created by partners Lorraine Picard and Ana Paula Chico, with natural beauty products for men and women.

Using organic and natural ingredients, the brand offers skincare and grooming products that are also cruelty-free and come in eco-friendly packaging. The selection includes lotions, shampoos, conditioners, scrubs and soaps for all skin types. Choose from single ingredients, such as cherry blossom or shea butter, or delicious combinations, like mint and sage, lavender and chamomile, and black amber and bergamot. You can also find aromatic candles, hair and body brushes and loofahs. And if you're struggling with jet lag, ask about their essential oils, which can help you relax and sleep better.

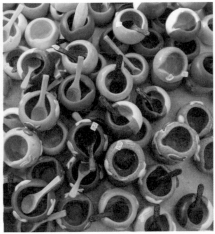

El Bazaar Sábado

*Classic and contemporary
Mexican crafts in a lovely
17th-century house.*

Plaza San Jacinto 11, San Ángel

Bombilla, line 1

Sat 10am–7pm

W

bazaarsabado.com

The ultimate showcase for Mexican creativity, this colourful market was founded in 1960 as a place where local craftspeople could directly interact with customers. Five years later, it found its current home in a 17th-century house, adapted by architects Manuel Parra and Ruth Rivera Marín (daughter of muralist Diego Rivera). Today the bazaar remains a platform for Mexican creators and also offers a contemporary line-up.

Walking the hallways means you can find a fascinating combination of all-time favourite crafts, such as stone kitchen tools – like molcajetes to make salsa – doll's house miniatures, and Nativity figures, as well as modern Mexican art and design, including lamps by Candela, jewels by Avocet, and clothes by Simona and Takamura. There are also spices and condiments by Beatriz Attolini and soaps and body mists by Remedios del Bosque. To recharge from shopping, there's a restaurant in the central courtyard that serves a casual buffet.

Markets + Shops

Cañamiel

Latin American designers are the stars at this sophisticated concept store.

Park Plaza, Av. Javier Barros
Sierra 540, Santa Fe

Mon–Sun 11am–6pm

$MXN

$500–$16,000

W

canamiel.com.mx

Fashion design graduate Nelly Navarrete launched this concept store in 2011 to create a home for exciting Mexican and Latin American designers. Since then, Cañamiel has become a destination for those seeking new, original trends.

You'll find Mexican labels, such as Sandra Weil's contemporary, feminine creations, plus she designs exclusive pieces for this store; Duo de Mar's chic resortwear; Mekuni's inventive shoes; Daniela Millán's dreamy jewellery; and Kiki's boho handbags, handmade by Maya artisans. International designers include Los Angeles–based Gladys Tamez, who creates gorgeous straw and cowboy hats, and a rotation of Brazilian and Argentinian talents.

The store's cool interior design, with raw concrete walls and a maze-like display structure, makes browsing fun, and the staff are knowledgeable. There's also a kids' section with cute ponchos, onesies and toys.

This mall also has a great contemporary Mexican restaurant: Cascabel, run by chef Lula Martín del Campo. Stop by for lunch after your shopping spree.

Mercado Jamaica

Flowers and plants from several states are displayed at this massive market.

Guillermo Prieto 45, Jamaica

Jamaica, lines 4, 9

Open Mon–Sun 24 hours

Feast your eyes on thousands of flowers of all colours, shapes and sizes at this market, which has been running since the 1950s. Among its more than 1150 stalls, you will find varied and beautiful plants and flowers from the Mexican states of Michoacán, Puebla, Chiapas, Oaxaca and Veracruz. It's a fascinating insight into local life, even if you can't take anything home from your travels.

It's always busy and sometimes a bit chaotic – in fact, cars and trucks drive inside the market, so watch where you're going. You're welcome to ask as many questions as you like, but note that not all sellers like you taking photos of their stalls, so ask politely.

Don't miss a walk around the flower arrangement hallways. You'll see elaborate creations for weddings and funerals, and there's also a food and vegetable section and awesome snack offerings. Many locals will tell you that the esquites (a warm cup of corn with cream, mayo, lime and chilli) alone are worth the trip.

Markets + Shops

*This colonial city's historic centre is a UNESCO World Heritage Site
and getting lost in its streets is a true joy. They say that Puebla has 365
churches – you could visit a different one every day for a year. It's also one
of Mexico's richest culinary destinations.*

There are a few churches in this beautiful city that you cannot miss, including the temple of **Santo Domingo** (Av. 5 de Mayo, Centro), where you'll find **La Capilla del Rosario**. Practically all of the interiors of this stunning chapel are covered in gold leaf, making it a perfect example of Baroque architecture during colonial times. Other Baroque constructions that are not to be missed are the **Temple of San Francisco** (Av. 14 Ote., Barrio del Alto), with its intricate brick and tile front, and the **Puebla Cathedral** (16 de Septiembre s/n, Centro), with an altar built by renowned architect Manuel Tolsá.

Make a stop at the **Biblioteca Palafoxiana** (Av. 5 Ote. 5, Centro), considered the first public library in the Americas. Built in the 18th century and decked with elegant cedar and white pine shelves, it holds a collection of more than 45,000 books, and while these can only be consulted by researchers, it's worth a visit because of its cultural relevance. And for a deep dive into the Baroque period, head to **Museo Internacional del Barroco** (Atlixcáyotl 2501, Reserva Territorial Atlixcáyotl), set in a striking modern building by Japanese architect Toyo Ito. The exhibitions inside will guide you along a journey through the architecture, painting, theatre and music of the Baroque.

Puebla is home to wonderful restaurants, including classics like **El Mural de los Poblanos** (16 de Septiembre 506, Centro) – perfect for trying timeless dishes, like mole poblano, made with dried chillies, chocolate, seeds and spices. For slightly more contemporary takes on local cuisine, try **Intro** (Atlixcáyotl 3246, San Martinito) by chef Ángel Vázquez, or the restaurant at **Casa Reyna boutique hotel** (Privada 2 Oriente 1007, Centro). Before you head back, stop for beautiful talavera pottery and tortitas de Santa Clara, the state's traditional cookies.

GETTING THERE

Approximate time and distance from Mexico City: two hours, 20 minutes (135 km/83 miles).

By bus: Leaving from Terminal de Autobuses de Pasajeros de Oriente (TAPO) bus terminal, you can travel with Estrella Roja (estrellaroja.com.mx) or ADO (ado.com.mx). While you can purchase your tickets at the station, it's better to buy them through the website a few days in advance.

Day tours: Capital Bus (capitalbus.mx) offers full-day tours with English-speaking guides. Check the website to book.

Driving: From the city centre, take Calzada Ignacio Zaragoza, which turns into the México–Puebla freeway. If you're in the southern part of the city, take Periférico until you reach the freeway.

One of the most important pre-Hispanic cities in Mesoamerica, this sprawling archaeological site (with a 264-hectare public access area) is known as 'the place where men became gods'. And it doesn't feel like an overstatement as you walk down Calzada de los Muertos, the city's main avenue.

Before you start your archaeological exploration, make sure you're armed with comfortable shoes, a hat, a nice layer of sunscreen and a bottle of water. Begin your stroll along the four-kilometre (2.4 mile) avenue **Calzada de los Muertos**, where you'll spot sites like **Atetelco**, **Tetitla** and **La Ventanilla**, which were used for residential purposes and boast murals with depictions of early life; and the grand **Pirámide del Sol**, the largest construction in the complex. Climb the 238 steps to the top but mind your step, as the surface is a bit uneven, and enjoy an incredible view from 64 metres (209 feet) high. The **Pirámide de la Luna** is smaller in scale – 43 metres (141 feet) but is built on higher ground and is located at the end of the Calzada, so it offers a privileged perspective of the entire complex, which was founded in 400 BC and built up until 300 AD.

Teotihuacán is also home to two specialised museums: **Museo de la Cultura Teotihuacana**, the site museum, and **Museo de los Murales Teotihuacanos Beatriz de la Fuente**, dedicated to the rich murals that brought this city to life.

Your cultural journey is surely going to leave you hungry, so head over to **La Gruta** (Circuito Arqueológico, Avenida del Puente s/n), located just off door five of the archaeological site, for a traditional Mexican meal – think tortilla soup and tacos – inside an actual cave. On weekends, it features performances by pre-Hispanic and folkloric dancers, too. If you plan on heading back to the city for lunch or dinner, bring snacks, as there are stands selling chips and candy (sweets), but nothing too nutritious.

To enjoy a truly breathtaking view of the complex, book a hot-air balloon about a month in advance, with **Sky Balloons** (skyballoons.mx), where you'll find tours for groups and couples. Keep in mind that it can get pretty windy, so this experience is more suitable for adventurous types.

GETTING THERE

Approximate time and distance from Mexico City: one hour (51 km/31 miles).
Day tours: Capital Bus (capitalbus.mx) offers an interesting half-day tour that leaves the city very early in the morning, allowing you to arrive at the site before the crowds. It will also take you to visit a local family's distillery for a tequila and mezcal tasting. Check the website to book.
Taxi or Uber: This is a convenient and safe way to get to the archaeological site. An Uber will usually charge you around $700 from the city centre, while a hotel taxi might be quite a lot pricier, depending on where you're staying.
Driving: Take the México–Pachuca freeway. After the Ecatepec toll booth, take the Teotihuacán exit. There is a public parking lot/carpark outside the site.

The laid-back vibes of this charming Morelos town have made it a favourite among Mexico City dwellers for years. Many believe that el Tepozteco hill – and the town in general – has a very strong, special energy, and in fact, Tepoztlán hosts spiritual and healing retreats all year long.

The main attraction in Tepoztlán is **Parque Nacional El Tepozteco**, a 24,000-hectare (59,305 acre) nature reserve that is home to dozens of interesting species, like orchids, lilies and small rabbits called teporingos, and is crowned by **la Casa del Tepozteco**, an Aztec temple built on top of **el Tepozteco** hill. Explore the site armed with good shoes and a large water bottle.

There's plenty to enjoy on lower ground, too. The town's market offers all kinds of colourful crafts – toys, embroidered shirts, musical instruments, as well as delicious food, like huauzontles (long, edible plants) stuffed with cheese and giant quesadillas. The surrounding streets are lined with cute little stores, coffee shops and bohemian bars. Take this chance to try pulque, an alcoholic drink made from fermented sap from the agave plant.

For a traditional Mexican lunch overlooking el Tepozteco, head to **El Ciruelo** (Av. Ignacio Zaragoza 17, Santísima Trinidad), where the menu includes crowd-pleasers like sopa de tortilla (tomato broth with fried tortilla strips, fresh cheese, avocado and cream) and fideo seco (thin noodles in a tomato and chilli sauce). Afterwards, head to the famous **Tepoznieves** (Av. Revolución 21, San Miguel) and choose from their dozens of ice-cream flavours, from classic coconut to aromatic rose petal.

GETTING THERE

Approximate time and distance from Mexico City: one hour, 30 minutes (90 km/55 miles).

By bus: Leaving from Central de Autobuses del Sur Taxqueña bus terminal, you can ride with ADO (ado.com.mx). While you can purchase your tickets at the station, it's smart to buy them through the website at least a few days in advance.

Taxi or Uber: An Uber will usually charge you around $1300 from the city centre, while a hotel taxi might be quite a lot pricier, depending on where you're staying. Keep in mind that you will have to make arrangements to get back, though, as there is no Uber service in Tepoztlán and a local taxi might not want to drive you back to the city.

Driving: Take the Ciudad de México–Cuernavaca freeway until you reach the Cuautla exit. Note that this freeway has some pronounced curves, so be sure to drive carefully.

In bloom since 2014, this is the largest floral park in the world, and it can provide you with a nice breather if you've had too much urban excitement in the city – it can happen.

These themed gardens have been carefully designed to create completely different atmospheres. The **Italian garden**, for example, is inspired by a Renaissance villa, with colourful flowers, cypress trees and classical fountains; while the tranquil **Japanese garden** has lakes, waterfalls and simple wooden constructions.

At the **cacti garden**, modelled after Mexico's desert landscapes, you can admire more than 200 species that thrive under extreme conditions, while the lush **tropical garden** will take you on a little journey to the country's rainforests. This section also houses a beautiful **orchid nursery**. There is a cool **maze** where you can get lost among walls of green, and a kids' area called **ConSentidos**, where kids can learn about sustainability and the environment through games and exhibitions.

There is a casual restaurant inside the park called **Jardines de México**, where breakfast and lunch are served buffet-style, but do bring snacks and plenty of water to keep yourself hydrated, as the weather here in Morelos is quite a bit warmer than it is in Mexico City. The good news is that you can visit Jardines de México all year long.

The entry fee is $275 for adults; $225 for seniors and children.

GETTING THERE
Approximate time and distance from Mexico City: two hours (137 km/85 miles).
By bus: Leaving from Central de Autobuses del Sur Taxqueña bus terminal, you can travel with Pullman de Morelos (pullman.mx) to the town of Puente de Ixtla. The bus ride will take a little less than two hours. At the station, take a taxi to Jardines de México. You should be there in about 20 minutes.
Taxi or Uber: An Uber will usually charge you around $1800 from the city centre, while a hotel taxi might be a lot pricier, depending on where you're staying. Do consider that you will have to make arrangements to get back, as there is no Uber service in the area.
Driving: Take the México–Acapulco freeway, and take the Taxco/Iguala exit. There is a parking lot/carpark at the gardens.

THE ESSENTIALS

Whether you have been to Mexico City before or you are a first-time visitor, here is some practical information that will help you with transport, etiquette and local knowledge.

GETTING TO AND FROM MEXICO CITY

Plane

Mexico City International Airport is one of the busiest international airports in the world and welcomes direct flights from major hubs in North and South America, Europe and Asia. Aeroméxico and Delta use Terminal 2, while all other airlines arrive and depart through Terminal 1.

You will spot authorised taxi companies at the two terminals, starting from the baggage claim area. Some of them include Yellow Taxi, Nueva Imagen, Sitio 300 and Porto Taxi. You'll pay at the airport depending on where you're going; they're completely safe and they operate 24/7.

To get a Metrobus (see below) from the airport, board at Door 7 of Terminal 1 or Door 2 of Terminal 2 and get on Line 4, to connect you with the centre of the city.

Bus

There are four main bus terminals: Central de Autobuses del Norte, Central de Autobuses Poniente, Terminal de Autobuses de Pasajeros de Oriente (TAPO) and Central de Autobuses del Sur, also known as Taxqueña. From here, you can travel to other towns and cities in the country. There are several bus companies, but the ones that offer routes to the most destinations and the best-quality travel are: ETN, ADO, Estrella Blanca and Estrella Roja.

GETTING AROUND MEXICO CITY

Authorised Taxi

During your stay in the city, always use authorised taxis. You can always ask the staff at your hotel/ restaurant to call one for you but avoid hailing one from the street, as they're likely to overcharge you if they see you're a foreigner (sorry). If you do hail one on the street, keep your eye on the meter.

Metrobus

This bus rapid transit (BRT) system is one of the most efficient means of transportation in the city. It has seven lines and more than 200 bus stops. They are mostly concentrated in the central neighbourhoods but can take you all the way to the city outskirts. A single trip will cost you $6 pesos. Pay for your card using the machines found at every station.

Metro

The subway system has 12 lines and 195 stations; it's quite efficient and it covers a great area of the city, although it doesn't reach some of the newer neighbourhoods, like Lomas de Chapultepec or Santa Fe. A single trip will cost you $5 and it uses the Tarjeta Recargable ticket (see below).

Ecobici

This eco-friendly bike-share system was installed a little more than a decade ago and has proven very successful. Registration is available at four offices in the city, or through the website (ecobici.cdmx.gob.mx), with just a valid ID and a debit or credit card. You can get a subscription for a year, a week, three days or only a day. The service is currently available in 55 neighbourhoods, with nearly 500 stations. If you want to give it a try, it's smart to do it in pedestrian-friendly areas, like Condesa or Polanco, and avoid the city's large and busy avenues, as traffic can be quite intense.

Tarjeta Recargable

This ticket card will allow you to use the Metro, Metrobus and Ecobici systems, so it's quite convenient if you plan to use them frequently. You can buy it using the machines found at every Metrobus station and recharge as needed.

Ride-share

Uber is 100% legal in Mexico and it's safe and quite affordable. Other ride-sharing options include Cabify and DiDi. You can always download one or two apps so as to have a few options during your stay.

MUSEUMS

Most museums in the city are closed on Mondays. Entrance to many of them is free on certain days of the week, so it's always smart to check out their schedules and plan your visit accordingly.

MEAL TIMES

On weekdays, meal times for most people revolve around their regular work schedule: breakfast around 9am, lunch at 2pm, and dinner around 8 or 9pm. On the weekend, there's no rush, and locals love to linger around the table. This means that we may have breakfast at 10am, and lunch can start at 3pm or maybe even 4pm, and if the conversation gets good, it can go on for hours. Dinner on the weekend usually begins at 9 or 9.30pm. Of course, most restaurants have very flexible hours and start serving lunch at 1pm or 1.30pm, and dinner at 7pm.

DIETARY REQUIREMENTS

At most restaurants and hotels, it's easy to ask for vegetarian, gluten-free or dairy-free options, but it's always better to check in advance, especially at places with tasting menus. The city has plenty of markets and convenience stores, so you can always pack a couple of snacks to be on the safe side.

TIPS

It's customary to tip between 10 and 15% in restaurants, coffee shops and bars. Tip your tour guides and the staff at your hotel, too ($50–$100 pesos for helping with your luggage, or any additional services, like bringing you a toothbrush or medication). You're not expected to tip cab drivers but do leave a little extra if they were especially efficient or friendly.

ETIQUETTE

From the moment you arrive, you'll notice that locals are warm and hospitable and they will appreciate the same attitude from visitors. A smile, a 'por favor' (please), and 'gracias' (thank you) will go a long way. Also, Mexican people are big on physical contact, so don't freak out if people you are meeting for the first time give you a hug or a kiss on the cheek! In terms of wardrobe, a pair of jeans and a nice shirt will make you feel comfortable in most settings, but fine-dining restaurants do call for nice dresses for women and jackets and ties for men. Sandals and open-toe shoes are OK, but avoid flip-flops unless you're going someplace extremely casual (locals hardly ever wear them).

SAFETY

As in most large cities of the world, there are some precautions to be considered while travelling in Mexico City.

- Keep your eyes on your belongings while out in crowded areas (especially cameras, mobile/cell phones and other valuable items) and leave your passport and some cash in a safe place in your hotel.
- If you find yourself in an area that feels unsafe or too empty (especially late at night), find a convenience store or a coffee shop from where you can call a cab or Uber to take you where you're going.
- Don't accept rides from unmarked taxis.
- If you're unsure about a certain area of the city that you're

THE ESSENTIALS

planning to visit, ask a local. Your hotel concierge, barista or store assistant will be happy to give you some tips that will help you feel safe.

WEATHER

Mexico City has mild weather all year long so it's a good destination for any season. During the winter it can get a bit chilly – with an average low of 6 degrees Celsius (42°F), while the warmest season starts in March and ends in June – with an average high of 26 degrees Celsius (78°F). It usually rains in the afternoons from June to September, while the fall (autumn) and winter bring clear skies.

PHONE SERVICE + WI-FI

If you want to use your phone freely, you can buy pay-as-you-go SIM cards from the three phone companies in the country: Telcel, AT&T and Movistar. You can buy the cards at convenience stores, such as Oxxo, 7-Eleven and Extra. Many public areas, like parks and plazas, have wi-fi but service is a bit inconsistent sometimes. You'll find that most hotels, restaurants, museums, coffee shops and bars have free wi-fi. Just ask for the password if needed.

PUBLIC HOLIDAYS

If you plan on visiting Mexico City on a holiday, you're in for a great time, as this usually means that you'll be witness to all kinds of fun celebrations, while restaurants, hotels and bars tend to offer special menus or events.

Do keep in mind, though, that some museums, restaurants or shops might be closed or working on a limited schedule on important public holidays like: 1 January, Easter Sunday, 1 May (Labor Day), or 25 December (Christmas Day).

Independence Day is 16 September and the celebrations begin at 11pm on the night of 15 September, when the president stands on the balcony of Palacio Nacional and calls out 'El Grito', honouring the words that Miguel Hidalgo, leader of the war of independence, pronounced back in 1810. Restaurants, bars and hotels all over the city hold patriotic-themed celebrations on that night, usually with plenty of food and drink to go around all night long. Día de Muertos is on 1 and 2 November and on this public holiday, Mexican people honour the dead by visiting them in cemeteries and setting up altars in their homes, which usually include photos of loved ones, candles, bright orange cempasúchil flowers and small reminders of things they liked (perhaps a glass of tequila). You can find beautiful altars in places like

THE ESSENTIALS

Zócalo (see p.143), Museo Dolores Olmedo (see p.153), or the Four Seasons hotel (see p.125), which will help you understand the fascinating relationship that our culture has with death. And don't forget to try pan de muertos (a fluffy, sweet bread covered in sugar) that is best paired with a cup of hot chocolate.

MONEY + ATMS

Local currency is the Mexican peso. While most businesses accept major credit cards (Mastercard and Visa, but some might not accept American Express), it's always smart to bring some cash with you, especially if you want to buy something cheap, like a street snack, a bottle of water or a small local craft. It's also good to take cash to markets.

ATMs are easy to find pretty much all over the city, and they will usually charge you around $32 for making a withdrawal. Make sure you use an ATM during the daytime and in a neighbourhood that feels safe to you. You can also find several money exchange bureaus at the airport, or head to a bank if you need to exchange money during your trip.

SPANISH

The city has been welcoming tourists from all over the world for years, so you should have no trouble getting by even if you don't speak Spanish. Most museums and art galleries – and many restaurants – have their information translated into English, as well as English-speaking staff. That being said, people really appreciate it if you try to speak a bit of Spanish, so here are a few basic words and phrases you can use:

Hola – Hello
Buenos días – Good morning
Buenas tardes – Good afternoon
Buenas noches – Good evening/ night
¿Cómo estás? – How are you?
Por favor – Please
Gracias – Thank you
Agua – Water
¿Cuánto cuesta? – How much is this?
No hablo español – I don't speak Spanish
Necesito ayuda – I need help
Dónde está el baño/la salida – Where is the restroom (toilet)/the exit?

The Essentials

GRACIAS

To Melissa, Megan, Alice, Lila and everyone at Hardie Grant for putting their talent and time into this book, and for trusting me with this incredible project. I wish I had a more creative way of saying this but all I can say is that this is truly a dream come true.

To my family and friends for being an endless source of love and support. Working on this book was as exciting and fun as it was challenging and, honestly, exhausting! Thank you for never letting me forget that I could do it, and do it well. Special thanks to those who came to explore the city with me (especially Ale, for tagging along on my very first and last expeditions!). To everyone who shared their suggestions and insights on their favourite spots. To my Aunt Guadalupe for her valuable knowledge, to Issa and Pedro for being my food gurus, and to Anaclara for always reading my stuff.

To the photographers who contributed with their beautiful images, especially the talented Tanya Chavez for taking my portrait during a particularly hot afternoon.

To the business owners, chefs, bartenders, store clerks, baristas, craftspeople, artists and designers whose passion brings Mexico City to life every day. This book exists because of you. This city is endlessly inspiring because of you.

Published in 2020 by Hardie Grant Travel,
a division of Hardie Grant Publishing

Hardie Grant Travel (Melbourne)
Building 1, 658 Church Street
Richmond, Victoria 3121

Hardie Grant Travel (Sydney)
Level 7, 45 Jones Street
Ultimo, NSW 2007

www.hardiegrant.com.au/travel

Copyright text and photography
© Cristina Alonso 2020
Copyright concept and design
© Hardie Grant Publishing 2020

A catalogue record for this
Book is available from the
National Library of Australia

Art and Fiesta in Mexico City
ISBN 9781741176452

10 9 8 7 6 5 4 3 2 1

Publisher
Melissa Kayser
Senior editor
Megan Cuthbert
Project editor
Alice Barker
Editorial assistance
Rosanna Dutson and Jessica Smith
Proofreader
Susan Keogh
Design
Oh Babushka
Prepress by Splitting Image Colour Studio

Printed and bound in China by LEO Paper Group

**All images © Cristina Alonso, except the
following:**

p. vi: Tanya Chávez; p. 39, p. 106, p. 152, p. 212
courtesy of Carlos Porraz; p. 113 courtesy of Bar
Oriente; p. 116 courtesy of Leonel Sámano; p.
129 (right) courtesy of St Regis Hotels; p. 133
(bottom left), p. 156 (bottom), p. 170 courtesy of
Alamy; p. 140 courtesy of Biblioteca Vasconcelos;
p 141 courtesy of Museo Memoria y Tolerancia;
p. 144 courtesy of Unsplash/Arpa Sarian; p. 145
courtesy of Papalote Museo del Niño; p. 134,
p. 146 (top) courtesy of iStock photos; p. 150
courtesy of Museo Soumaya/Fundación Carlos
Slim; p. 153 courtesy of Museo Dolores Olmedo;
p. 172 courtesy of Museo Tamayo; p. 184 courtesy
of MUAC; p. 206 courtesy of LoredAna; p. 214
courtesy of Daniela Morfín; p. 216 courtesy of
Jardines de México; p. 224 (portrait of Cristina
Alonso) courtesy of Tanya Chávez.

Mexico City map and illustrations © Shutterstock
2020

Disclaimer: While every care is taken to ensure
the accuracy of the data within this product, the
owners of the data (including the state, territory
and Commonwealth governments of Australia)
do not make any representations or warranties
about its accuracy, reliability, completeness or
suitability for any particular purpose and, to the
extent permitted by law, the owners of the data
disclaim all responsibility and all liability (including
without limitation, liability in negligence) for all
expenses, losses, damages (including indirect or
consequential damages) and costs which might be
incurred as a result of the data being inaccurate or
incomplete in any way and for any reason.

Publisher's Disclaimers: The publisher cannot
accept responsibility for any errors or omissions.
The representation on the maps of any road or
track is not necessarily evidence of public right of
way. The publisher cannot be held responsible for
any injury, loss or damage incurred during travel.
It is vital to research any proposed trip thoroughly
and seek the advice of relevant state and travel
organisations before you leave.

Publisher's Note: Every effort has been made
to ensure that the information in this book
is accurate at the time of going to press. The
publisher welcomes information and suggestions
for correction or improvement.